YOUR
KINGDOM
COME

UNLOCKING THE MIRACULOUS
THROUGH FAITH AND PRAYER

DANIEL KOLENDA

Daniel Kolenda
Your Kingdom come
Unlocking the Miraculous through Faith and Prayer
English

ISBN 978-1-933446-29-5
Copyright © 2013, Daniel Kolenda

Edition 2, Printing 1

Unless otherwise indicated, all Scripture quotations are taken from the *King James Version* of the Bible.

Scripture quotations marked NKJV are taken from the *New King James Version* of the Bible.
Copyright © 1979, 1980, 1982, Thomas Nelson, Inc., Publishers.

Scripture quotations marked AMP are taken
from *The Amplified Bible, New Testament*, copyright © 1958, 1987, by The Lockman Foundation, La Habra, California;
or from *The Amplified Bible, Old Testament*, copyright © 1964, 1987 by Zondervan Publishing House, Grand Rapids, Michigan.

Scripture quotations marked NASB are taken from the *New American Standard Bible*.
Copyright © 1960, 1962, 1963, 1968, 1971, 1972, 1973, 1975, 1977, 1995 by The Lockman Foundation. Used by permission.

Scripture quotation marked NEB (The New English Bible) is taken from
The Word – The Bible from 26 Translations, Curtis Vaughan, Th. D., Gen. Ed., Mathis Publishers, Inc., Gulfport, Mississippi,
copyright © 1988, 1991, 1993.

Editor: Brad Braland
Cover Design: Joe DeLeon
Layout: Roland Senkel
Photographs: Oleksandr Volyk
Rob Birkbeck
Special Thanks to: Dr. John Shiver

Published by:
Christ for all Nations
P .O. Box 590585
Orlando, Florida 32859
U.S.A.

www.cfan.org

Contents

Dedication

*Dedicated to the Christ for all Nations partners worldwide
who faithfully bombard Heaven for our team in prayer.*

Introduction

Their years with the Master had taught the disciples one thing about Jesus ... He was a man of prayer. Whether in the middle of the day or in the middle of a conversation, it was common for Jesus to steal away to a quiet place where He could have uninterrupted communion with His Father. Jesus loved His disciples, He loved the multitudes, and He loved fellowship and ministry, but nothing was more important to Him than His relationship with His Father.

We know that prayer was a priority for Jesus because what is practiced by the teacher will be imitated by the student. And when the disciples came to Jesus with one request, they didn't say, "Lord, teach us to preach." They didn't say, "Lord, teach us to cast out demons." They said, "Lord, teach us to **pray**." Others may have asked, "Jesus, what is the secret to Your ministry?" But the disciples already knew and within them grew a burning desire to understand it more. "Lord," they said, "teach us to pray."

This secret of Jesus' ministry has also characterized the lives of great men and women of God throughout history who discovered the incredible power of prayer. John Wesley said, "God does nothing, but in answer to prayer."[1] The great pioneer missionary Adoniram Judson was known to withdraw from his friends and family seven times a day to be alone in prayer.[2] David Brainerd once wrote, "I love to be alone in my cottage where I can spend much time in prayer."[3] John Hyde was a missionary to India who earned the name John "Praying" Hyde for his remarkable life of devotion. When his health began to fail, he visited a doctor in Calcutta who made a startling discovery; John "Praying" Hyde's heart had shifted in his chest as a result of years of grueling intercession.[4] The list goes on and on.

It comes as a shock to many Christians that there is anything to learn about prayer. Some think prayer is simply chattering to an invisible man. They think they know all there is to know about the subject like a man who thinks he knows everything about the Atlantic because he has dipped his toe in the surf!

The disciples had been faithful and observant Jews all of their lives, and as such, prayer was something they had practiced continually since childhood. But once they had observed Jesus' life of devotion, they recognized that there were depths of prayer they had never fathomed and there was much to be learned; thus, the request, "Lord, teach us to pray. Teach us not to recite memorized words or fulfill a religious duty. Teach us to touch heaven and to impact the earth. Teach us to be fervent and effectual, to move mountains, to break chains, to cast out demons, to heal the sick, to raise the dead, to impact cities and nations, to change the course of history and bring heaven to earth. Teach us to really, really, really **pray**!"

I am an evangelist who works on the front lines of the battle for souls in some of the most difficult, dangerous, and remote locations on earth. This book comes not from a marble writing desk, but from the dusty trenches where lives hang in the balance. For us, prayer is not a luxury or an accessory – it is a matter of survival. The prophet Jeremiah spoke of a dreadful day that is fast approaching when multitudes of lost souls will declare with eternal regret, "The harvest is over, the summer has ended, and we are not saved." As the clock counts down the final hours before the end of the age, it is the heart of God that none should perish, but all should come to repentance that motivates us to go into all the world and preach the gospel (see 2 Peter 3:9).

Although my primary emphasis as a minister is evangelism, I have written this book because there is an increased urgency in my spirit and a growing awareness that God desires to raise up a mighty army of intercessors in the earth in these last days to spark a prayer revolution that will touch the world.

I also believe that the mass evangelism movement and the prayer movement, which have arisen almost independent of one another, must come together if we are to accomplish the purpose God has for us.

Without intercession covering the work of the evangelists, they will not have the steam in their engines to reap this gigantic harvest that is now ripe and ready. Without evangelism and real world impact, intercession lacks purpose and relevance. But together they are a dynamic and revolutionary combination that has the potential to change the world!

This book is for those who desire to enter into a divine partnership with God and His purposes by joining the prayer revolution. It begins with the disciples – you and me – sitting at the feet of Jesus in the School of Prayer. It begins with a simple request: "Lord, teach us to **pray**!"

1

DISTURB US, LORD!

Be sober, be vigilant;
because your adversary the devil, as a roaring lion,
walketh about, seeking whom he may devour.

1 Peter 5:8

The pounding at the door seemed to rattle the entire house just before the foot of an impatient Roman soldier kicked it from its hinges. Peter was still in bed and half asleep when the guards grabbed him and hauled him out into the dusty Jerusalem streets where a prison wagon was waiting. Roughly, they thrust him into the crowded carriage ribbed with iron bars and there, in the faint light of early dawn, Peter recognized the tired faces of his fellow inmates. It was his friends: Andrew, James, John, Philip, Thomas, Matthew, James (the son of Alphaeus), Thaddeus, Simon, Matthias, and Bartholomew the other apostles of the Lamb and the original founders of the Church.

The high priest had exercised his political power and commanded that these disciples of Jesus be rounded up like ordinary criminals to be incarcerated in a common prison. But with the evening would come an extraordinary miracle. Acts 5:19 says, *"But the angel of Lord by night opened the prison doors, and brought them forth."* What a glorious deliverance! What an incredible testimony! God had demonstrated His power once again, and these early followers of Jesus must have felt invincible.

A LETHAL ENEMY

I think what happened next is typical of human nature. It would appear that in the midst of great victories, a sleepy cloud of complacency had dulled some of the believers' spiritual senses.

In Acts 12 we read that the persecution against the Church continued. But this time it was Herod who had initiated the arrest and instead of seizing all the apostles at once, he started with just one – James, the brother of John. Everyone assumed that James would be fine. After all, God had delivered the apostles from prison once before, and surely He would do it again … or would He? We read of no prayer meetings, no vigils, and no intercession. All was well and no one was concerned until the tranquility was shattered and the Church was devastated by the dreadful news: James was dead, executed at the hands of the wicked ruler.

Complacency is one of the most dangerous enemies of the believer because it is so easy to fall into and, like a vivid dream, it is very difficult to detect in our own lives before we are rudely awakened. God is so good and faithful to us in His mercy. But it is easy to take His faithfulness for granted in the good times and confuse presumption for faith.

Someone once said, "Complacency is a blight that saps energy, dulls attitudes, and causes a drain on the brain. The first symptom is satisfaction with things as they are. The second is rejection of things as they might be. 'Good enough' becomes today's watchword and tomorrow's standard. Complacency makes people fear the unknown, mistrust the untried, and abhor the new. Like water, complacent people follow the easiest course – downhill. They draw false strength from looking back."[5]

In nations, in individuals, in families, and in business, complacency has the same effect; it is the enemy of victory and the ally of defeat. In no other area is complacency so lethal as in the prayer life – especially when everything is going well.

Utter Dependence

I must have prayed for weeks before I preached my first sermon at 14 years of age. I pleaded for God's help and blessing, knowing that without it I would be a miserable failure. Today I often preach more than twelve times in a single week. I no longer feel nervous, even when preaching to crowds of hundreds of thousands, and therein lies the danger. Although I feel comfortable and confident behind the pulpit, I must continually remind myself that my sense of security is just an illusion. I could preach the most articulate sermon with the most extraordinary delivery, but I would still be a miserable failure without the blessing of the Lord.

> Complacency is the enemy of victory and the ally of defeat.

I find that the more secure we feel, the more danger we are in, because it is in comfort that we can so easily forget our utter need for God. That's why, before I get up to preach, I pray the prayer that used to be said in the classrooms of America before prosperity made her apathetic towards the very One who had so blessed her: "Almighty God, I acknowledge my utter dependence upon You and beg for Your blessing." It is this awareness of our complete dependence upon God that will make us diligent in prayer. If you lack this consciousness in your life, chances are you are sleepwalking through the perilous wilds of complacency.

"Wake up o sleeper, rise from the dead, and Christ will shine on you."

Ephesians 5:14 (NIV)

In Amos 6:1 AMP the prophet declares, *"Woe to those who are at ease in Zion, and to those on the mountain of Samaria who are careless and feel secure."* The children of Israel had grown apathetic in their prosperity and comfort. They had lost their sense of urgency and were not concerned about the things of God. But their perceived security was a myth. The mercy of God that held back disaster was stretched to the limit, and in verse 7 NASB God says the party is over! *"Therefore, they will now go into exile at the head of the exiles, and the sprawlers' banqueting will pass away."* Only after disaster had struck and the nation found itself in the chains of captivity did it turn to the Lord again.

God forbid that we should have to be shaken out of our complacency by tragedy or disaster. How much better it would be if we would remain vigilant in prayer, recognizing that even in the good times, *"your adversary the devil, as a roaring lion, walketh about, seeking whom he may devour"* (1 Peter 5:8).

In 1577 Sir Francis Drake wrote:

> *Disturb us, Lord,*
> *When we are too pleased with ourselves,*
> *When our dreams have come true,*
> *Because we dreamed too little,*
> *When we arrived safely,*
> *Because we sailed too close to the shore.*

Disturb us, Lord,
When with the abundance of things we possess,
We have lost our thirst for the waters of life;
Having fallen in love with life,
we have ceased to dream of eternity,
And in our efforts to build a new earth,
We have allowed our vision
of the new heaven to dim.[6]

Everybody seems to want "revival," thinking it is a pleasant and enjoyable experience. But to be revived is to be shaken out of a state of slumber, to be jolted out of apathetic complacency, to be alarmed, awakened, and startled. Too many churches praying for revival have a "Do not disturb" sign hanging on the door. Revival that fits neatly into a comfortable cradle is not revival at all. Instead of praying for revival, perhaps we should pray with Sir Francis Drake, "Disturb us, Lord!" Powerful prayer begins where complacency ends.

> Too many churches praying for revival have a "Do not disturb" sign hanging on the door.

"Therefore let us not sleep, as do others; but let us watch and be sober."

1 Thessalonians 5:6

II

PRAYER THAT OPENS DOORS

The effectual fervent prayer
of a righteous man availeth much.

James 5:16

O nce James had been murdered, Herod's religious Jewish contingent was thrilled with his initiative and applauded him. Suddenly he saw an easy way to gain favor with a party that had always given him such opposition. Acts 12:3 AMP says, *"When he [Herod] saw that it was pleasing to the Jews, he proceeded further and arrested Peter also."*

This time things would be very different. The tragedy of James' death had shaken the believers to the core and all potluck dinners were cancelled – it was time to pray. The Scripture is careful to preface the story of Peter's deliverance with the following state-ment: "[fervent] *prayer was made without ceasing of the church unto God for him"* (Acts 12:5). This statement is very significant, because the writer of Acts is trying to show us that the miracu-lous deliverance to follow would be a direct result of those fervent and persistent prayers that were offered up by the believers.

It was the last night of Passover week and Peter was chained between two menacing soldiers. This was to be his last night on earth, for in the morning he would be executed as James had been just a few days earlier. But the Bible says that *"suddenly"* a light from heaven illuminated that gloomy prison house as an angel of the Lord appeared in his cell. He smacked Peter on the side and said, "Get up quickly!" An interesting fact is found in Acts 12:7. It tells us that Peter's chains, *"fell off from his hands"*! Notice that it does not say that the angel broke the chains off Peter's hands, but simply that they fell off.

The angel said to Peter, "Put your clothes on and follow me." They walked past the first set of guards who didn't notice him. They walked past the second set of guards who also seemed oblivious to his escape. Then they approached the most obstructive barrier of all – a huge iron gate that separated the prison from the street. This gate was designed to protect the outside world from the dangerous criminals it confined. It was an obstacle that seemed totally insurmountable, but Peter was not worried – he thought it was just a dream anyway.

You will notice that verse 10 says that when they reached the gate, it *"opened to them of his own accord: and they went out, and passed on through one street."* Only then did the angel vanish, and suddenly Peter realized that it was not a vision. He had actually been delivered!

THE INVISIBLE HAND

Can you see the theme that is emerging here? In the story, every obstacle, every barrier, and every obstruction is completely impotent. The chains fell from Peter's hands, the guards could not see him escaping, and finally the iron door opened and the most amazing part is that all of this seems to have happened almost by itself. Although a mighty angel is sent to escort Peter out of the prison, the angel does not touch the chains, the guards, or the doors – they seem to be impacted by an invisible hand.

> Intercession is a privilege that belongs exclusively to man

We see very clearly from what is emphasized in verse 5 that it is because of the prayers of the saints that all this is happening. "[Fervent] *prayer was made without ceasing of the church unto God for him."* The prayers of the believers were the power that loosed the chains, removed the obstructions, and opened even the most impenetrable doors.

> God has given man not only the authority but also the responsibility to influence events in the earth for His glory

It was Peter to whom Jesus said, *"And I will give unto thee the keys of the kingdom of heaven: and whatsoever thou shalt bind on earth shall be bound in heaven: and whatsoever thou shalt loose on earth shall be loosed in heaven"* (Matthew 16:19).

Oh, my friends, if we had any idea of the incredible power that is available to us through prayer, I think we would find it so easy to heed Paul's prompting to *"pray without ceasing"* (1 Thessalonians 5:17).

INTERCESSION BELONGS TO MAN

Our prayers are one vehicle through which God has chosen to impact the world. John Wesley once said, *"God does nothing but in answer to prayer."* Intercession is a privilege that belongs exclusively to man. (No angel can intercede on our behalf nor can the angels intervene in earthy affairs according to their own will.) God has given man not only the authority but also the responsibility to influence events in the earth for His glory.

Intercession is such an important function, the Bible tells us that at this present time it is the role of Jesus Himself – He is continually making intercession for us. The office of the intercessor can only be filled by man, and Jesus is not an exception to the rule. Remember that He is now and will forever be not only fully God, but also fully man. It is awe-inspiring to think that throughout all of the ageless eons of eternity, Jesus was a divine, non-physical being, who was a part of the uncreated, eternal Godhead. Then the Holy Spirit overshadowed Mary and impregnated her with the seed of Christ. From that moment throughout the rest of eternity, He became, remains, and will forever be a God/Man.

> Intercession is not only the privilege of man, but it is also our sacred duty.

In Luke 22:69 Jesus said, *"Hereafter shall the Son of man sit on the right hand of the power of God."* Jesus is now glorified. He is seated at the right hand of the Father. He is a part of the Godhead – yet He is still a man. In fact, He still chooses to identify Himself explicitly as "the Son of Man."

The Scriptures are very clear that His body is a glorified, **human** body that still bears the scars of His human experience and it always will. He wears the scars on His hands, feet, and side like a wedding ring that will forever remind us of His love. I'm sure that He could have the scars removed to have a perfect, unblemished body, but to Him they are His most flattering features and He wears them proudly. When Jesus stepped down, it was an eternal transition. He will never again be the same as He was before His condescension.

A song by Joan Osborne came out when I was a teenager. The chorus says, "What if God was one of us ... just a stranger on the bus trying to make His way home?" What Joan didn't understand is that God **was** like one of us. He experienced all of the same difficulties and temptations and discomforts that we have, plus much more than we will ever understand. He was like us. But what is more is that He **is** like us. He has chosen to relate to us on this most intimate of levels for all eternity, and His manhood is the credential that qualifies Him to be a merciful and faithful High Priest in things pertaining to God.

If intercession is so important that Jesus Christ Himself has made it His primary role, the significance of this calling seems quite obvious. Intercession is not only the privilege of man, but it is also our sacred duty, and Jesus, as the "firstborn among many brethren" leads us by example.

> As long as the enemy can keep the people of God convinced that they are powerless against the circumstances they face, their impact in the earth will be anemic.

EXPLOSIVE PRAYER

Reinhard Bonnke once said, *"Man needs God but God needs man. When the two come together for God's purposes, anything becomes possible."* The supernatural agreement through faith between Almighty God and a man or a woman who knows how to pray is more powerful than a thermo-nuclear bomb! It is a partnership between heaven and earth that is exercised when God's people agree with the purposes of God and pray those purposes into being in the earthly realm. This largely unrecognized truth from God's Word is what James 5:16 was referring to when it says, *"The effectual fervent prayer of a righteous man* [or woman] *availeth much."* The Amplified Bible translates this same scripture, *"The earnest* [heartfelt, continued] *prayer of a righteous man makes tremendous power available* [dynamic in its working]." The word "power" in this scripture comes from the Greek word *dunamis* which properly translated means power, inherent ability, capability, ability to perform anything. This word *dunamis* derives from the same root word from which we get the word "dynamite," a powerful explosive![7] The Bible teaches us that when we pray, we have the potential of igniting the explosive dynamite of heaven in our circumstances and in the events of the earth.

Prayer prayed in faith has the power to destroy the devil's schemes and make the way for every barrier to be shattered, every gate to be blown open, and for God's blessings to flow without interruption. That's power! Whenever there is an agreement between two or more people who are united in faith, petitioning heaven for the same thing, the *dunamis* power of heaven that is released is multiplied exponentially!

As long as the enemy can keep the people of God convinced that they are powerless against the circumstances that they face, their impact in the earth will be anemic and of little influence. But that is not what God has in mind for His people. There's much, much more.

III

PRAYER MATTERS

Thus saith the LORD;
Cursed be the man that trusteth in man,
and maketh flesh his arm,
and whose heart departeth from the LORD.

Jeremiah 17:5

I n the beginning of Acts 12, before Luke recounts in detail the story of Peter's release from prison, you will notice he starts by mentioning that Herod had just executed James. It seems that he is setting the two events in juxtaposition to one another, the only difference being prayer. What if the church had prayed for James as they had prayed for Peter? Is it possible that the story could have ended differently?

Does prayer really make a difference? Can we really alter the outcome of situations and circumstances through prayer? Someone once said that prayer doesn't change things, it only changes the person praying, but this is contrary to Scripture. Prayer **does** change situations because God has made us partners with Him for the fulfillment of His purposes in the earth and prayer is one fundamental way in which we partner with God.

The prophet Elijah is a great example of this principle. For three years and six months Israel had been plagued by famine until God promised the prophet that He would send rain.

> *"And it came to pass after many days, that the word of the Lord came to Elijah in the third year saying, 'Go show thyself to Ahab and I will send rain upon the earth.'"*
>
> 1 Kings 18:1

But at the end of the same chapter in which the promise was given, we see Elijah praying for the fulfillment of the promise. He cast himself down on the ground and put his face between his knees. Seven times he sent his servant to look for any sign of rain and in the meantime James 5:17 tells us that he *"prayed earnestly"*. One might wonder why Elijah needed to pray at all if God had already promised that He would send the answer. But Elijah understood that the promise required partnership through prayer. Oh how many promises there are to the Child of God who will only take a hold of them earnestly through faith and prayer. Yes! Prayer does matter. It has the power to change the world.

STANDING IN THE GAP

Ezekiel 22:30-31 says *"And I sought for a man among them, that should make up the hedge, and stand in the gap before me for the land, that I should not destroy it: but I found none. Therefore have I poured out mine indignation upon them; I have consumed them with the fire of my wrath: their own way have I recompensed upon their heads, saith the Lord GOD."*

> Prayer is one fundamental way in which we partner with God.

This passage was written in the days when men fought battles face-to-face, sword-to-sword and hand-to-hand. There are many ancient legends of small bands of men and in some instances, a single man, standing in a narrow passage and holding off an entire army single handed; as in the famous story of the lone Viking who brought the whole Saxon army to a halt at Stamford Bridge or the legend of the Roman hero Horacius who withstood the Etruscan army and saved Rome. If the walls of a city were breached in battle, a warrior would consider it his greatest moment of glory to stand in that narrow gap, face the enemy and defend the entire city behind him. But God says in Ezekiel 22:30 that when He looked for a man to stand in the breech, he found none. Where were the warriors? Where were the intercessors? When the wall is breeched what could possibly be more important than standing in the gap?

The enemy is constantly working to penetrate the walls of our lives and invade the Church of Jesus Christ. We see the effects of this onslaught every day; a man of God falls into sin, a family is torn apart, a church is split, someone becomes ill, etc. Yet how often the people of God stand on the sideline watching the catastrophe and enthusiastically exploiting their new conversation piece. But God is not pleased. We have not been called to gossip and gawk, but to jump into the gap, to make up the hedge and to defend the breech! Our failure to "make up the hedge and stand in the gap" can have dire consequences. That's why prayer is such a serious issue. It is a matter of life and death. And one man or woman, strategically positioned in prayer can be used by God to bring about mighty victories for His glory!

Unto the Glory and Praise of God

We live in a physical world, where temporal material needs can often seem overwhelming and perpetual in our narrow view of reality. But in the grand scheme of eternity our problems are actually very small and insignificant.

Consider this: if you looked out of the window of an airplane at 30,000 feet on a clear day you would see how even the largest,

31

most imposing man-made structures on earth would be hardly visible much less impressive at that altitude. But actually, in terms of the universe, it would still be an incredibly close distance (only about 5.7 miles away).

Looking up at the stars on a clear night, it is mind-blowing to think that the closest one (after the sun) is 25 trillion miles from earth!

While that sounds like a vast distance, completely impossible for our finite minds to comprehend; it is actually relatively close – slightly more than four light-years[8] away.

Compare that with other stars that are known to be more than 80,000 light-years away and there could be as many as 400 billion of them – just within our galaxy!

If you feel small now, hold on to your hat! **There are hundreds of billions of galaxies** in the observable universe, **which spans tens of billions of light-years!**

Just try for a moment to comprehend, how small you are. When you look down at the earth from 30,000 feet, (not even a nanosecond compared to the light-years we use to measure the universe) human beings are not even visible – and now we are talking about billions of light-years!

In the context of the universe, the earth itself is less than an infinitesimally microscopic speck of dust and we are the earth's microbes.[9]

But there's more, because all the unfathomable vastness that makes up our universe exists in a tiny plane of time and space that we know as the physical world. Isaiah 57:15 says that God inhabits eternity; a realm of infinite scope in which our entire cosmos is only a drop of water in an endless ocean.

My friend, no matter how daunting your problem or need may seem right now, be assured that in reality, it is a small matter of very little true significance. Why should the omnipotent, omnipresent, omniscient, eternal God intervene in our affairs of such utter triviality? Because God uses our lives as a platform from which He desires to receive praise and glory. From the day we are born until the day we die, our lives exist for one reason – to glorify God.

Why do our problems matter? Because through them God can be glorified. It is easy to become self-centered in prayer focusing on our own needs and desires, but ultimately, even if we benefit from an answered prayer, it is not about us – it is all about Him! The philosophy of the age is the spirit of humanism, which teaches that the chief end of all being is the happiness of man. We are led to believe that this also applies to our relationship with God; that His chief goal and purpose is to make us happy, healthy, wealthy and comfortable. But Scripture teaches the opposite. Revelation 4:11 says that we were created for God's pleasure! 1 Corinthians 6:20 says, *"For ye are bought with a price: therefore glorify God in your body, and in your spirit, which are God's."*

Take divine healing for example; every person who is supernaturally healed is still going to die one day, so someone might ask,

33

"What is the point?" The real purpose is that God might receive praise as a result. For this reason, our problems **do** matter and have eternal significance; because God's glory is a matter of eternal importance.

In John 9:2 NASB the Disciples asked Jesus about a man who was born blind, *"saying, 'Rabbi, who sinned, this man or his parents, that he should be born blind?'"* and in verse 3, *"Jesus answered, 'It was neither that this man sinned, nor his parents; but it was **in order that the works of God might be displayed in him.'"***

The disciples wanted to know if this situation was about the blind man or maybe his parents, but Jesus made it clear – it wasn't about any of them. It was about bringing glory to God!

Scripture tells us about a few books that are in heaven. One is called "The Book of Life." Another is called, "The Book of Remembrance." There are also other books mentioned in Revelation 20:12. I think one of God's books must be a picture album. In this book there are thousands of small snapshots of moments in human history. I think there is a picture Noah building the Ark. There is a picture of God making His covenant with Abraham. There is a picture of Jacob wrestling with the Angel of the Lord. There is a picture of Moses leading the Children of Israel out of Egypt. There is a picture of Peter walking on the water. Perhaps there is a picture of something that happened in your life as well. All these pictures are snapshots of moments in time when a man or a woman dared to trust God. They are moments when someone obeyed even when they didn't understand. They are snapshots of moments when someone was faithful even unto death. They are snapshots of when God's strength was made perfect through human weakness.

A hundred trillion years after this earth has been melted down and everything we know as "reality" has vanished forever; your best and worst moments, your struggles and victories, your pains and pleasures will seem like a faded dream. In that day, the only memorial of our world will be the snapshots in God's picture album and every one will have the same caption, "Unto the Glory and Praise of God." These are the things that really matter. Our feelings, emotions, wants, desires and pleasures are ultimately meaningless compared to God's eternal glory. This is why we pray. This is why we intercede. Not just so that our temporary lives can be enriched, but so that God's enduring kingdom may be advanced.

> This is why we intercede.
> Not just so that our temporary lives can be enriched, but so that God's enduring kingdom may be advanced.

35

The King who Dug his own Grave

There's an old hymn that says,

> *Oh what peace we often forfeit*
> *Oh what needless pain we bear*
> *All because we do not carry*
> *Everything to God in prayer.*

It's amazing how many people choose to involve God so little in their lives. When it comes to decisions about business, family, career and the weightier matters of life, they seek out qualified counsel, yet they never bend a knee before the King of the Universe who stands by longing to help them. He desires to be glorified through our lives yet many times we deprive Him of that right.

It is more than just unfortunate when we fail to inquire of the Lord. When we rob our Creator, Sustainer and Provider of His rightful place in our lives, it is literally offensive to God.

2 Chronicles 16:9 AMP says, *"For the eyes of the Lord run to and fro throughout the whole earth to show himself strong in behalf of those whose hearts are blameless toward Him."* This is a verse that is often quoted in many different situations, but it may surprise you to learn the context of that verse and the fascinating circumstances surrounding it. It is both an insight and an admonition for our own lives.

Baasha, the King of Israel came up against Judah in war and tried to starve the people out by besieging them at Ramah. So Asa, the King of the besieged Judah, *"brought silver and gold out of the treasuries of the house of the Lord and sent them to Ben-hadad king of Syria … saying, 'Let there be a league between me and you … break your league with Baasha king of Israel, that he may withdraw from me.'"* (2 Chronicle 16:2-3).

The Syrians, whose allegiance Asa had bought with gold from the Lord's house came down and rescued the southern kingdom from the hand of Baasha. It would seem like a happy ending, but the Lord was not pleased. God wanted to be Judah's defender and deliverer, but instead Asa had given that opportunity to the Syrians. In the same way Asa had taken the gold from the Lord's house and given it to another, he had also taken the glory from the Lord and given it to another.

So God sent a prophet named Hanani to king Asa with this message, *"because you relied on the king of Aram* [Syria] *and not on the LORD your God, the army of the king of Aram* [Syria] *has escaped from your hand. Were not the Cushites and Libyans a mighty army with great numbers of chariots and horsemen? Yet when you relied on the LORD, he delivered them into your hand.* **For the eyes of the LORD range throughout the earth to strengthen those whose hearts are fully committed to him**. *You have done a foolish thing, and from now on you will be at war."* (2 Chronicle 16:7-9 NIV)

Because of fear, Asa chose to call upon, and put his trust in, the king of Syria rather than on the Lord and God was offended. As a result of this, the Lord gave Asa over to the very thing he feared most, *"from now on you will be at war."* By not including the Lord, Asa had actually brought upon himself the very thing he was trying to avoid. *"It is better to trust in the LORD than to put confidence in man. It is better to trust in the LORD than to put confidence in princes."* (Psalms 118:8-9)

How often has God stood by ready, willing and able to help us, but we never turned to Him or gave Him an opportunity to intervene and bring glory to Himself through our crisis. As a result we have often forfeited peace and struggled under the load of unnecessary burdens – all because we did not inquire of the Lord. What's worse, an opportunity to bring glory to God was lost.

What is so amazing is that Asa makes the **very same mistake** again only 3 verses later:

*"In the thirty-ninth year of his reign Asa was diseased in his feet – until his disease became very severe; **yet in his disease he did not seek the Lord, but relied on the physicians**. And Asa slept with his fathers, dying in the forty-first year of his reign."* (2 Chronicle 16:12-13 AMP)

Can you see the pattern? The author is trying to communicate a moral through this story that is of utmost importance. Asa called upon the help of foreign armies instead of the Lord and as a result he inherited perpetual war. He called on the aid of doctors, instead of the Lord, when he became sick and as a result he inherited death. God wanted to help Asa. God wanted to deliver him from his enemies. God wanted to heal him from his diseases. But for some strange reason, like so many of us, Asa ignored God in the issues that mattered most and as a result he sealed his own fate.

The final verse of the chapter sums Asa's life up with an almost contemptuous caption: *"And they buried him in his own tomb* ***which he had hewn out for himself.****"* In essence, Asa dug his own grave and put the final nail in his own coffin because he insisted on calling upon the arm of flesh rather than on the Lord. God was insulted by Asa's disregard and gave him over to that which he feared most. Jeremiah 17:5 says, *"Thus says the LORD, 'Cursed is the man who trusts in mankind And makes flesh his strength, and whose heart turns away from the LORD.'"*

We find a similar story in 2 Kings 1 where king Ahaziah fell through a lattice in his upper chamber and was injured. He sent messengers to the Philistine city of Ekron to ask their god, Baal-zebub, whether or not he would recover.

"But the angel of the LORD said to Elijah the Tishbite, 'Arise, go up to meet the messengers of the king of Samaria and say to them, ***Is it because there is no God in Israel that you are going to inquire of Baal-zebub, the god of Ekron?*** *Now therefore thus says the LORD, 'You shall not come down from the bed where you have gone up, but you shall surely die.'"* (2 Kings 1:3-4 NASB)

Ahaziah's failure to inquire of the Lord was a serious offense to God that cost him dearly.

I wonder how many Christians are suffering today because they didn't trust in and seek the Lord in the midst of their trial. Faith often seems like the more difficult option. It is so much easier to trust a lawyer, a doctor, a colleague, a counselor or even our own selves. But after trusting in all of these other things, so many people find themselves given over to the very thing that they fear and in that moment they cry, "Why God!?" Don't wait until your wheels have fallen off before you cry out to the Lord. Seek the Lord while He may be found and call on Him when He is near (Isaiah 55:6). View your difficulty as merely an opportunity for the Lord to receive Glory.

GOD'S ETERNAL GLORY

> Perhaps the daunting circumstances you are facing are just a platform from which God desires to demonstrate a mighty miracle to an unbelieving world.

Peter's imprisonment was a crisis that could have ended in catastrophe or victory. To the believers gathered in Mary's house praying for his release, their primary concerns were most likely immediate. They were frightened that they would lose the great apostle who was also their friend and leader. They were probably empathetic with Peter's suffering and the brutal execution he was facing. But there was a more enduring matter at stake – the eternal glory of God. The intercessors probably had no idea that through their prayers God would unleash His power in an extraordinary way that would be a testimony to many generations – including ours. How many thousands have been inspired by this amazing story? Yet, it might have been a tragic tale lost to history had it not been for the prayers of those few fervent prayer warriors standing in the gap.

God is primarily concerned with receiving glory from our lives. Perhaps the daunting circumstances you are facing are just a platform from which God desires to demonstrate a mighty miracle to an unbelieving world. The eyes of God are going to and fro throughout the earth looking for someone through whom He can show himself mighty. He wants to receive glory through your sickness. He wants to receive praise through your financial emergency. He wants to receive honor through your family situation. Call upon the Lord. Inquire of Him. Ask Him what He thinks and desires. Don't deprive Him of the opportunity to be your "very present help in trouble." Don't lean on the arm of the flesh ... don't dig your own grave.

IV

PRAYER THAT DELIVERS

Behold, the LORD's hand
is not shortened, that it cannot save;
neither his ear heavy, that it cannot hear.

Isaiah 59:1

God wants to answer our prayers of intercession more than we want Him to answer them. Intercession is not a human invention – it is God's idea! He has called us to partner with Him in prayer. God longs to reveal His great power in cities, regions, and nations in order that multitudes of people may be saved. He wants to reveal Himself to those who walk in darkness that they may behold the glorious light of the gospel and come to Him. He longs to see hell plundered and heaven populated!

He has given His people (the Church) all the tools we need through prayer and faith in the mighty name of Jesus to see that happen if we will only use them as He has intended. He has put into our hands the keys of the kingdom that are capable of unlocking the treasure houses of heaven, shattering the chains off of nations, destroying yokes, and breaking curses.

BREAKING THE CURSES

We have seen this so often in our massive Gospel Campaigns around the world. In many of the African villages where we minister, the people have lived in fear of certain curses and demonic principalities that have kept them in bondage and terror for generations. Often these strongholds have names familiar to every local inhabitant, but the people dare not say them aloud for fear of the demon powers behind them. When we come for one of our Gospel Campaigns, we challenge these forces with the power of the cross. We ask that a list of the local curses be provided and then through the massive sound system we begin to pray, calling out the curses and breaking them by name, one by one, in the name of Jesus! After each curse is broken, a mighty "Amen" rises from the crowd and a palpable sense of freedom and joy causes the people to dance and sing.

In one city, the witch doctors practiced their divination by standing on certain "sacred" stones that they claimed would speak to them. After our campaign, the witch doctors began to complain, "The stones no longer speak." Through prayer we have the power to overcome the enemy and to break every chain.

Out of a horrible Pit

The year was 1919. My great grandfather had immigrated to America eleven years earlier and settled in the city of Pigeon, Michigan, where he pastored a German church that had grown from small meetings in his rural home.[10] Growing up, I often heard the story of Matis Nagi, whose testimony had left an indelible impression on the minds of all who knew him. His wife was a faithful member of my grandfather's congregation, but darkness lived inside the heart of Matis that set him at odds with God and the church which he hated passionately.

From time to time, a strange power would come over him and he would be driven to do bizarre things. He was known to throw himself down from the loft of his barn headfirst without harm. It was apparent to everyone that demonic activity was at work in his life, and many times the church leaders warned him to no avail. My Uncle John[11] said that he had told Matis, "The way you have chosen will lead you to destruction. You are in danger of being possessed by the devil fully. Stop this and humble yourself before God so you can receive help." But he would not listen.

One evening after an argument, in a fit of rage, Matis gave himself over to the power that had been influencing him for so long. All the events to follow would be completely blotted from his memory, as the demonic power possessed him completely.

Mrs. Nagi had gone to the city to shop and when she returned at dusk on her horse-drawn wagon, she could see the silhouette of her husband standing on the porch in the shadows holding an axe in his hands. As she drew closer, a feeling of uneasiness came over her. Something was not right. Her anxiety turned to terror when she saw that her husband was covered in blood and his eyes were hollow and empty. She immediately rode away to the house of my grandfather.

> Intercession is not a human invention – it is God's idea. He has called us to partner with Him in prayer.

47

"Come quickly," she pleaded. When Matis saw my grandfather and the elders of the church approaching the house, he began to cry out in fear. He was mumbling cryptic phrases about how he saw them as being covered in red and could not come near them. And then in a moment, he ran away and disappeared into the forest. Together Mrs. Nagi and the elders entered the house where they made the grizzly discovery. Matis had brutally murdered his mother and three children in cold blood.

The news of the grizzly act spread like wildfire through the small farming community, which was gripped by terror. Farmers would accompany their wives to the barns to milk the cows and would not go into the fields to work for fear of the deranged demoniac that lurked in the woods.

Sometime later, the police finally apprehended Matis and took him to the jail, but he was so violent and uncontrollable that he had to be isolated in a cell by himself. Inside the jail, he tore all his clothes off and sat naked. He shouted terribly in his sleep and had to be prevented from killing himself.

The judge determined that he was so thoroughly insane that he was not fit to stand trial, so he was committed to an insane asylum a hundred miles away in Pontiac, Michigan.

The doctor sent word to Mrs. Nagi that her husband was incurably sick and that his condition was worsening each day. He feared that her husband would soon die and said that she should come immediately.

It was a very trying time for the believers in my grandfather's church, and when my Uncle John arrived at the memorial service, he was met by Mrs. Nagi who said, "How sad it is that I have been robbed of my beloved children – the saddest of all is that my husband has become the prey of Satan and Satan is the victor."

"No, Sister Nagi," he said, "Satan is not the victor! This seeming victory is only temporary. There is no doubt that the grandma who loved the Savior is now safe with Him. The same applies to the little children. And concerning your husband, there is hope to wrestle him from the power of Satan through prayer and faith. This we will do in the name of Jesus."

The congregation shook themselves out of their despair and set themselves to pray. My Uncle John later wrote, "We all fell on our knees and prayed with fervor to God that He might destroy all attempts of Satan that even this tragedy will turn to triumph and that He also might deliver the possessed one from the power of Satan. Heaven seemed to open up for us. We were filled with a holy joy and with courage of faith so that we commanded the demonic spirits to disappear and to leave the possessed one in the name of Jesus. I remember very well how I was filled with a Holy Spirit given assurance of faith, and I shouted to the praying believers, 'Brothers and Sisters, it is finished! God has listened to our prayer. We can proclaim by faith that the possessed one is delivered.'"

It was my Uncle John who went to visit Matis in the asylum. Upon arrival, he was escorted to the office of the head physician, Dr. Christian. The doctor was silent for a while and then he said, "I do not understand this case. Three days ago I wrote a letter to the wife of this man and explained to her that according to our tests her husband was incurably sick and probably would not live much longer. Yesterday morning a change took place, and it is so radical that his condition seems to be completely normal. Well, whatever this is," he said, "it seems that a miracle has happened here."

Dr. Christian rang the bell for a guard who escorted Uncle John to the visiting room. After a few minutes, Matis was ushered in. When he saw Uncle John, he rushed up to him, "Please tell me what has happened!" he begged. "I cannot believe what these people have told me!" The previous day, when Matis had suddenly and instantly come to his senses, he had no recollection of any of the events that had transpired. As Uncle John told him the whole story, Matis broke down and sobbed, overwhelmed with grief. He had loved his children very much and had been especially close to his dear elderly mother. "O Lord, have mercy on me … a sinner!" he cried. "I am the worst man who exists!"

50

It's difficult to see how a story like this could have a happy ending, but God in His incredible mercy has a way of bringing triumph out of even the worst of tragedies. Matis had been used by Satan as a tool of destruction, and he would live with the unimaginable pain of this knowledge for the rest of his life. But through the power of prayer, Jesus broke the chains off of his mind like the demoniac of Gadara and set this captive free. Through the miraculous deliverance, something had changed in Matis' spirit. He repented of his rebellion, surrendered to Jesus Christ, and became a true child of God. Not only was he delivered of demonic possession, but he was saved and filled with the Holy Spirit.

The doctors found this dramatic recovery so unbelievable that they were compelled to keep him in the asylum for more than a year under careful observation before giving him a clean bill of health. He was released and lived the rest of his days with his family as a faithful follower of Jesus – a changed man.

Uncle John recalled that more than 20 years later when passing through Detroit, he was preaching in a particular church and the believers were asked to testify of what the Lord had done in their lives. A little elderly man stood up and said, "If anyone has a reason to praise the Lord it is me." It was Matis, now old and grey. He had lived many years with the regret of his past, but he was overflowing with thankfulness to the God who had shown him such incredible mercy.[12]

With tears streaming down his face, he began to quote Psalm 40:2-3: *"He brought me up also out of an horrible pit, out of the miry clay, and set my feet upon a rock, and established my goings. And he hath put a new song in my mouth, even praise unto our God: many shall see it, and fear, and shall trust in the LORD."*

THE LONG ARM OF THE LORD

In our mass Gospel Campaigns where hundreds of thousands attend each meeting, multitudes of sick and needy people gather for prayer. It is physically impossible to lay hands on each person, but we have made an incredible discovery. There are no limitations with God. When we pray over the gigantic crowd, miracles and healings begin to pop up like popcorn, and from the front to the back the power of God flows equally to all. Often, we have physically cut chains off of the hands and feet of

> Jesus broke the chains off of his mind like the demoniac of Gadara and set this captive free.

51

insane people who have been delivered miraculously through the simple power of faith and prayer.

Do you have loved ones who are bound by the power of Satan? Do you want to see salvation come to your children, grandchildren, parents, brothers, and sisters? Do you have a friend who is addicted to drugs, alcohol, or a perverse lifestyle? Have you tried to reach them with no success? You have a secret weapon.

My friend, it's time to pray. Through prayer the *dunamis* power of God can apprehend that person right where they are, shatter the chains that bind them, open their prison doors, and bring deliverance, freedom, and healing. You may be separated by thousands of miles, but distance is no difficulty for the omnipresent Holy Spirit.

> You can have a real impact that reaches to the ends of the earth without ever leaving home.

Isaiah 59:1 NEB says, *"The Lord's arm is not so short that he cannot save"*. Although Peter was imprisoned on the other side of town, through prayer in the name of Jesus, the physical chains on his hands were loosed and all barriers were removed.

Matis Nagi was in an asylum a hundred miles away, but through prayer, the chains wrapped around his mind were loosed, deliverance came to his soul, and his life was transformed.

When you pray, you have the power to bring deliverance to the oppressed. You can have a real impact that reaches to the ends of the earth without ever leaving home. What you bind on earth will be bound in heaven – what you loose on earth will be loosed in heaven. No door, no chain, no barrier, and no distance are too great for the long arm of the Lord!

V

PRAYING UNDER AN OPEN HEAVEN

Oh that thou wouldest rend the heavens,
that thou wouldest come down,
that the mountains might flow down at thy presence,
as when the melting fire burneth,
the fire causeth the waters to boil,
to make thy name known to thine adversaries,
that the nations may tremble at thy presence!

Isaiah 64:1-2

One of the most remarkable prayers of intercession recorded in the Bible is found in Isaiah 64 where the prophet calls upon the Lord, saying, *"Oh, that You would rend the heavens and come down, that the mountains might quake at Your presence – as fire kindles the brushwood, as fire causes water to boil – to make Your name known to Your adversaries, that the nations may tremble at Your presence!"* (Isaiah 64:1-2 NASB).

The word "rend" literally means to tear or to tear open.[13] Isaiah was crying out to God that He would "tear open" the heavens and show Himself to the world that the world might see Him as Isaiah had seen Him! Isaiah's passion is seen in his expression, "Oh."

There is something deeply embedded in the heart of every person who longs to personally know and experience God. There is an "Oh" within us all. That desire which grows from within is but a reflection of the fact that man was originally created in the image of God and designed with the capability of personally knowing and experiencing God.

Saint Augustine said, "For thou has made us for thyself and our hearts are restless until they find their rest in thee." This longing of the heart is an integral part of the basic fabric of the human personality. It is expressed in the art, music, customs, and beliefs of every culture around the world that go back as far as the earliest evidences of recorded history.

When sin entered the world, man, who had been designed to live in unbroken fellowship with God, was suddenly separated from the One he had been designed to walk with in perfect harmony for all of eternity. A barrier that divides two worlds, the natural and the supernatural, appeared because of Adam's sin that separated the physical realms of fallen mankind from the spiritual realms filled with all of God's richest presence, power, and blessing.

In this prayer for God to "rend the heavens and come down," I believe that Isaiah was reflecting upon a previous experience in his life, recorded in Isaiah 6:1-8, in which he had been caught up into heaven and received the commission and anointing for his life and prophetic ministry. He recalls it, saying, *"In the year that king Uzziah died I saw also the Lord sitting upon a throne, high and lifted up, and his train filled the temple"* (Isaiah 6:1).

Isaiah continued in the following verses to describe his experience in God's presence. He spoke of angelic beings about the throne crying out, *"Holy, holy, holy, is the Lord of hosts: the whole earth is full of his glory"* (v.3). He spoke of the visible manifestation of God's glory. He described his sudden and overwhelming awareness of sin when he stood in the magnificent presence of the holiness of God. He thought he would surely die in such a holy place where he had suddenly found himself! But he also found grace there, and his sin was purged with holy fire. It was in this place that his life and destiny were forever changed. He would never be the same again!

Pay careful attention to what the angels were crying to one another. Notice, they did not say, "heaven is full of His glory." Rather, they said, "The **earth** is full of His glory." This was a prophetic insight into a time that is coming of which Scripture says, *"For the earth shall be filled with the knowledge of the glory of the LORD, as the waters cover the sea"* (Habakkuk 2:14).

When Isaiah prayed for God to rend the heavens and come down, he was asking for the fulfillment of the prophetic promise he had received in his vision many years earlier. He was saying in essence, "Lord, if the earth is going to be filled with Your glory, You must rend the heavens and come down!" Isaiah realized that this "rending of the heavens" would be necessary for God to fulfill His plan for this world.

THE STAIRWAY TO HEAVEN

59

The Gospel of John is distinctly and wonderfully different from its three synoptic counterparts. Some have speculated that John wrote his Gospel long after Matthew, Mark, and Luke and that John had not only the opportunity to read what the others had written, but he also had many years to reflect on his own experiences in light of what had been recorded. As an old man, under the divine unction of the Holy Spirit, John was convinced that there were still some essential things that needed to be said, so he set out to tell the rest of the story in his own words.

John is an unashamedly biased reporter who writes with irresistible persuasion He openly states his objective in chapter 20, verse 31, when he says, *"But these are written, that ye might believe that Jesus is the Christ, the Son of God; and that believing ye might have life through his name."* Everything in John's Gospel is strategically incorporated to convince the reader that Jesus Christ is the Son of God, because John knew that through this knowledge we could receive eternal life.

It is incredible that while John omits the story of Jesus' nativity, baptism, temptation, and transfiguration, he uses nine verses in the opening chapter to tell us a seemingly insignificant story about a young man named Nathanael. But a closer look will reveal that this otherwise untold account is a profound and luminous thesis from which John's exceptionally convincing argument will springboard in the following chapters of his Gospel.

The next day He purposed to go into Galilee, and He found Philip. And Jesus said to him, "Follow Me." Now Philip was from Bethsaida, of the city of Andrew and Peter.

Philip found Nathanael and said to him, "We have found Him of whom Moses in the Law and also the Prophets wrote – Jesus of Nazareth, the son of Joseph." Nathanael said to him, "Can any good thing come out of Nazareth?" Philip said to him, "Come and see."

Jesus saw Nathanael coming to Him, and said of him, "Behold, an Israelite indeed, in whom is no deceit!" Nathanael said to Him, "How do You know me?" Jesus answered and said to him, "Before Philip called you, when you were under the fig tree, I saw you." Nathanael answered Him, "Rabbi, You are the Son of God; You are the King of Israel."

Jesus answered and said to him, "Because I said to you that I saw you under the fig tree, do you believe? You will see greater things than these."

And He said to him, "Truly, truly, I say to you, you will see the heavens opened and the angels of God ascending and descending on the Son of Man."

John 1:43-51 NASB

In order to understand what is happening here, I am going to ask a series of key questions about the text, and from it a wonderful revelation will emerge.

WHAT'S GOING ON WITH THE FIG TREE?

The fig tree may seem like an oddly reoccurring theme here, but the cultural context reveals that there is more than meets the eye. In the rabbinic tradition, a fig tree is often used as a metaphor of the Torah (the first five books of the Old Testament). Nathanael may have been sitting under it literally or figuratively, but either way it seems clear that he was studying the Scriptures. When Jesus said that he saw Nathanael under the "fig tree," He was indicating that He saw Nathanael reading the Torah, which leads us to the second question.[14]

WHAT IS IT THAT NATHANAEL WAS STUDYING IN THE TORAH?

Of course, in Nathanael's day, there were no chapter and verse distinctions that we have in our modern Bibles, but I believe it would have been somewhere around chapter 28 of Genesis. He would have been reading about his ancient ancestor, Jacob (whose name means deceiver)[15] who stole his brother's birthright,

61

defrauded his elderly father, and escaped with his life. He would have read how Jacob reached Bethel where he rested for the night. There Jacob laid his head upon a pillow of stone and had a dream. *"And he dreamed that there was a ladder set up on the earth, and the top of it reached to heaven; and the angels of God were ascending and descending on it!"* (Genesis 28:12 AMP).

You will notice that before Nathanael met Jesus, he was a hardened skeptic who asked in reference to Jesus, *"Can anything good come out of Nazareth?"* But somewhere between verses 46 and 49, he dramatically converted to a convinced believer who declared to Jesus, *"Rabbi, You are the Son of God; You are the King of Israel"* (John 1:49 NASB). And this incredible transformation seems to have happened almost instantly, which leads us to ask a third question.

WHY THE SUDDEN CHANGE OF HEART?

Nathanael was clearly dumbfounded by Jesus' astonishing depth of prophetic insight.

First, Jesus had demonstrated that He knew that Nathanael had been studying the scriptures before Philip called him, which it seems was hidden knowledge.

Second, Jesus knew exactly what Nathanael had been studying and alluded to it when He called Nathanael *"an Israelite indeed"* (a descendant of Jacob, the "deceiver," whom Nathanael had just been reading about) *"in whom is no guile* [or deceit].*"*

And third, by this same statement, Jesus proved that He knew not only **that** Nathanael had been studying the Torah **and** exactly **what** he had been studying in the Torah, but the clincher was when Nathanael realized that Jesus saw something no one could possibly see – the very heart itself.

This demonstration so moved Nathanael that he declared his faith in Jesus, *"Rabbi, thou art the Son of God; thou art the King of Israel."* And that is when Jesus made **the most incredible statement of all** – it was the punch line of John's story. *"Because I said unto thee, I saw thee under the fig tree, believest thou? thou shalt see greater things than these"* (v.50).

And then Jesus alluded back to the scripture that Nathanael had been reading about Jacob and made a clear reference to the story of Jacob's ladder: *"Truly, truly, I say to you, **you shall see the heavens opened and the angels of God ascending and descending on the Son of Man**"* (John 1:51 NASB).

In essence, Jesus said, "Nathanael, are you impressed that I read your mail? Are you impressed that I knew you were reading about Jacob's ladder? Oh, Nathanael, I've got something better for you. Wait until you see that **I AM Jacob's ladder!**"

Jesus declared Himself to be more than a prophet, more than a Rabbi, more than a political deliverer, and more than a king. He declared Himself to be the bridge between heaven and earth, the link between God and man, the portal that God has opened on earth, giving us direct access to heavenly realms.

This is only the first of many such revelations about the identity of Jesus that John includes in this book. For instance, Jesus says:

I am the living bread that came down out of heaven (John 6:51).
I am the light of the world (John 8:12).
I am the door (John 10:7).
I am the good shepherd (John 10:11).
I am the resurrection and the life (John 11:25).
I am the way, and the truth, and the life (John 14:6).
I am the true vine (John 15:1).
Truly, truly, I say to you, before Abraham was born, I am (John 8:58).

John seems to be shouting to us what Philip shouted to Nathanael:

"We've found Him ... the One Moses and the prophets wrote about ... the One who solves all the riddles, the One who answers all the questions!"

We've found Him:
   The way, the truth, the life
   The bread of life
   The light of the world
   The door
   The good shepherd
   The resurrection
   The vine
   The great I AM

He is the Passover lamb.
He is the Ark of Noah's salvation.
He is the brass serpent lifted up in the wilderness.
He is the rock of Horeb.
He is the city of refuge.
He is the veil in the tabernacle and the tabernacle itself.
He is the unleavened bread and the manna from heaven.
He is our Melchezideck.
He is our kinsman-redeemer.
He is our high Priest.
He is the tree of life.
He is the stairway to heaven.
He is the second Adam.
He is Isaac going to get a bride.
He is the warrior standing before Joshua with a drawn sword.
He is Jonah three days and three nights in the heart of the earth.
He is in every way the fullest and most complete fulfillment
and source of every promise,

> *every type,*
> *every shadow,*
> *every epiphany,*
> *and every theophany.*

He is the end of all theology.
He is the reason for every genealogy.
He is at the heart of every prophecy.
His coming has split history in two and has changed absolutely
everything!

Isaiah's Prayer answered

> He declared Himself to be the bridge between heaven and earth, the link between God and man, the portal that God has opened on the earth, giving us direct access to heavenly realms.

Many people still pray Isaiah's prayer for God to rend the heavens and come down, pleading despondently like a beggar dejectedly crying for a piece of bread. But my friends, the good news is that the prayer of Isaiah was answered 2,000 years ago! God truly did rend the heavens and came down through Jesus Christ. Could there be a more dramatic rending than the one that happened at Calvary? The earth was split, the veil in the temple was rent from top to bottom, and the precious body of Jesus Christ was broken in order that heaven might invade the earth.

On Him the angels of God ascend and descend for us. Through Him all the resources of God are poured out and the needs of humankind can be met. By Him, man can be reconciled unto God and the wrath of God has been appeased.

God has rent the heavens and has come down. He has destroyed that ancient barrier between heaven and earth, and today all the riches and resources of God are available to the one who will take them by faith through prayer.

Hebrews 10:19-22 says:

Having therefore, brethren, boldness to enter into the holiest by the blood of Jesus,
By a new and living way, which he hath consecrated for us, through the veil, that is to say, his flesh;
And having an high priest over the house of God;
Let us draw near with a true heart in full assurance of faith, having our hearts sprinkled from an evil conscience, and our bodies washed with pure water.

God wants us to approach Him in prayer with assurance and confidence in His all-sufficient provision. Today we can march boldly into the presence of God with a pure conscience and a heart full of faith, knowing that God has already destroyed everything that stands between Him and us by the blood of Jesus Christ. He truly has given us the keys to the kingdom of heaven.

> Today all the riches and resources of God are available to the one who will take them by faith through prayer.

Through prayer we put this incredible power into action. Someone once said, "Prayer is the lifelong opportunity of a lifetime." The prayer of Isaiah has been answered. God has rent the heavens. Now let's bring heaven to earth!

VI

PRAYER THAT BRINGS HEAVEN TO EARTH

Thy kingdom come.
Thy will be done in earth,
as it is in heaven.

Matthew 6:10

Jesus prayed in Matthew 6:9-10 NASB, *"Our Father who is in heaven, hallowed be Your name. Your kingdom **come**. Your will be done, on earth **as it is in heaven**."*

Jesus taught us to pray that all the glory of His Father's kingdom would break through and be manifested on the earth, bringing the transference of all of heaven's purposes and blessings into the earthly arena.

Many years ago I had a most interesting vision. I saw a massive dam. It was holding back a mighty river on one side, but on the other side was thirsty ground, parched and cracked in the sun. I understood that the river represented the glory of God, and the parched ground represented the world. I knew that it was God's will that the knowledge of His glory cover the earth as the waters cover the sea, and so I said, "Lord, how will Your glory breach that massive wall?" Then I saw it. Tiny broken places began to form in the dam … hairline fractures that seemed so insignifi-

cant. But out of those tiny cracks, razor sharp spurts of water began to spray through. The cracking continued and I watched as small chunks of the wall began to fall away. Soon water was gushing in from all sides, and suddenly, in one moment, the mighty dam was swept away and the parched ground was covered. Then the Lord spoke to me and said, "My glory will cover the earth through broken people."

> Then the Lord spoke to me and said, "My glory will cover the earth through broken people."

Suddenly, I saw Jesus at the Last Supper breaking the bread of communion, and He said, *"This is my body, which is **broken** for* *you"* (1 Corinthians 11:24). When Jesus spoke of His body being broken, He was speaking of the crucifixion.

Immediately the words of the Apostle Paul in Galatians 2:20 NASB came flooding into my spirit: *"I have been crucified with Christ; and it is no longer I who live, but Christ lives in me; and the life which I now live in the flesh I live by faith in the Son of God, who loved me and gave Himself up for me."* What a powerful confession! To be crucified with Christ – this is the brokenness that will result in His life flowing out through ours to the dry and parched world around us. *"It is no longer I who live, but Christ lives in me."*

> It is in this laying down of our own will and desires that our prayers become truly powerful.

When we are broken, like Gideon's clay jars, the light of Christ inside will shine out, and those rivers of living water inside of us will come pouring out as Jesus promised they would. But how can we be crucified with Christ? Should we find a band of Roman soldiers and ask them to nail us to a cross? The reality is that Jesus had laid down His life long before He was nailed to the cross. Hear Him praying in the garden, *"Not my will, but thine, be done"* (Luke 22:42). This is true brokenness. It's where the real crucifixion takes place, and it is in this laying down of our own will and desires that our prayers become truly powerful.

Psalm 51:17 says, *"The sacrifices of God are a broken spirit: a broken and a contrite heart, O God, thou wilt not despise."*

PRAYING ACCORDING TO THE WILL OF GOD

One of the greatest hindrances to the true revelation of the glory of God in the earth is prayer offered by those who have personal agendas that seek to exalt themselves. They pray, "Not thy will, but mine, be done." God sees absolutely everything. He hears every prayer, but He also looks deep within the heart of the individual who prays the prayer, and clearly understands the motivations of the heart which are behind it!

> To be crucified with Christ – this is the brokenness that will result in His life flowing out through ours to the dry and parched world around us.

Nothing is ever concealed from His eyes. Prayer of any sort for anything is always going to be subject to His scrutiny. He not only hears what we petition Him to do, but He also sees all – the true reason that the petition is being made. This is what James was referring to when he said:

*"You lust and do not have. You murder and covet and cannot obtain. You fight and war. Yet you do not have because you do not ask. You ask and do not receive, because you ask amiss, that **you may spend it on your pleasures**"* (James 4:2-3 NKJV).

God loves it when we pray the things that are on His heart more than our own. One of the highest purposes of prayer and intercession is to help bring His kingdom into the earth so that He will be glorified. The truth is clearly illustrated by Jesus when He said, *"And whatever you ask in My name, that I will do, that **the father may be glorified in the son**. If you ask **anything** in My name, I will do it"* (John 14:13-14 NKJV).

73

Many people have attempted to use faith and prayer in the name of Jesus as a blank check to get whatever they want for themselves. God has given us wonderful promises about asking, believing, and receiving. That is not in dispute whatsoever, but there is a higher calling in faith and prayer. It is to ask for things, that when given, will be used exclusively to bring glory to our Heavenly Father through His Son, the Lord Jesus Christ! It's a type of prayer that is not about us, but it is all about Him and **for** Him. This is the kind of prayer that God desires. Jesus has promised that if we pray that way and with that motivation, *"If you ask **anything** in My name, I will do it"* (John 14:14 NKJV).

In 1 John 5:14-15 NKJV, we find another wonderful promise of scripture. It reads as follows: *"Now this is the confidence that we have in Him, that if we ask anything according to His will, He hears us. And if we know that He hears us, whatever we ask, we know that we have the petitions that we have asked of Him."*

> God loves it when we pray the things that are on His heart more than our own.

One of the great secrets of prayer is the discovery of the unlimited power that is available when God's people begin to intercede for things that God has clearly promised in His written Word. Faith and expectancy in intercession are little more than presumption and delusion if they are not firmly rooted in that which is the expressed will of God to perform. Thank God that because of His great love, mercy, and grace, He doesn't give us everything we ask for. If He did so, many times disaster would be the result for us as well as the abortion of His purposes and plans!

God is absolutely honest. He can never lie. He will never promise things that He is unable or unwilling to deliver. We can have absolute, unwavering confidence that when we go to Him in prayer, seeking those things that we know are His expressed will to give and to do, a revelation of His glory and power will soon come. It will never fail. When we know that we know that we know what the will of God is, we can pray that will with the unwavering assurance that the answer is on the way.

When we begin praying for a mighty outpouring of the Holy Spirit that will break the devil's back and glorify God, the heavens will begin to leak under the weight of His glory. When we begin to passionately pray that souls be saved and that the name of the Lord Jesus be famous in the nations, we can be absolutely confident that heaven is beginning to move in response. Jesus has promised that when we pray with the motivation that His Father be glori-fied, He will respond by doing **anything** that we ask Him to do!

> When we begin praying for a mighty outpouring of the Holy Spirit that will break the devil's back and glorify God, the heavens will begin to lead under the weight of His glory.

When we begin to pray, "Not my will, but thine, be done," our lives become a crack in the wall that allows the glory of God to flow to the earth. The Scriptures declare that one day the knowl-edge of this glory will completely cover the earth like the waters cover the sea. There could not be a more thorough saturation. Although this prophetic promise is still unfulfilled, we have seen many glimpses of what happens when God's people pray.

THE DIVINE ALLIANCE

Charles Finney (1792-1875) is considered by many people to have been one of the greatest revivalists in American history. When Finney preached in a city, the entire region was powerfully impacted by the holy presence of God, which seemed to descend like a cloud. The tangible presence of God would be felt for miles around and multitudes of people would come to Jesus as if being drawn by a mysterious, magnetic force. Churches would be over-whelmed with new converts. Crime rates would plummet, and jails would empty because of the numbers of people who had come to Jesus. The moral nature of cities and regions would be impacted for decades to come because of the supernatural work that was done by the Holy Spirit through this man of God. Interestingly, approximately 80 percent of those people who came to Jesus in Finney's meetings were still actively serving the Lord 25 years after their initial salvation experience[16] – an extraordinary statistic.

The amazing revivals that followed the ministry of Charles Finney were much more than just the result of the eloquent preaching of this evangelist. There was an atmosphere that followed Charles Finney that reflected the holiness of God. When people encoun-tered that atmosphere, their testimony was much the same as the prophet Isaiah who, encountering the holiness of God, cried out in despair, *"Woe is me! for I am undone"* (Isaiah 6:5). People were stricken by the horrors of their sins and the deep offense that sin caused in the heart of God. A reverential fear of the Lord was experienced by many that caused them to turn to the Lord with true, heartfelt repentance, and they were never the same again.

Much has been written about the amazing ministry of Charles Finney, but very little is known about another man named Daniel Nash who was an associate of Finney. Very few people even knew that he existed. He was very quiet by nature and rarely, if ever, attended any of the revival meetings where Finney preached. Though he had been a pastor early in his life, he had been wounded by some church leaders who had fired him from his church thinking he was too old. He was 46 at the time. This breaking of Nash's heart was only a part of the preparation for a much greater work that God had prepared for him to do. Nash's ministry was a ministry of prayer and intercession. Because of his hurt, he withdrew from public ministry but became a man of mighty prevailing prayer!

God brought Daniel Nash and Charles Finney together to form a team that was to be used by God in a most phenomenal way. Nash would precede Charles Finney's arrival in a city for revival meetings. He would go to the city and check into a boarding house and begin praying for the meetings that were coming. Sometimes he wouldn't come out of his room for days at a time as he devoted himself totally to intercession. Sometimes people reported hearing weeping and groaning coming from this man's room as he prayed for the Holy Spirit's power to be released and a mighty harvest to be reaped when Charles Finney came to preach.

Daniel Nash would pray for days before he felt that the work had been done in the spirit for the meetings to convene. Other times he would pray for three to four weeks in advance of Finney's arrival, but he would not quit until he felt in his spirit that the preparation through intercession was complete. Nash prayed until he felt that the spiritual atmosphere had been prepared, and once he felt a release, he would send word to Charles Finney that the town was ready for him to come. Finney would follow, preach the gospel, and the tidal floods of God's holy, convicting, and saving glory would overwhelm the town and people would come to Jesus to be saved as a result.

The greatest moves of God in American history occurred during this season of time. Entire regions were changed as a result of Finney's ministry. Historians point to those meetings as having such a profound impact upon people and societies that the effects could still be seen a century or more later![17] The powerful preaching of Charles Finney that saw hundreds of thousands of people saved would have never had the impact it did had it not been for the spiritual partnership with the intercessory ministry of Daniel Nash. It is interesting to note that only four months after Daniel Nash's death, Charles Finney left the itinerate revival ministry to pastor a church. The powerful revivals that characterized his ministry and changed a nation began to wane.

Daniel Nash is buried in a simple grave in an obscure cemetery behind a farmer's barn in upstate New York. It was lost in history for many decades. On his small, well-worn tombstone are these words: "Daniel Nash – prayer minister for Charles Finney." Though he was virtually unknown to the masses, God used Nash in a most profound way to birth the revivals of Charles Finney which touched multitudes. Surely Daniel Nash enjoys the same fruit of reward as Charles Finney in heaven today because of the role he played in intercession and prayer!

I believe that there are many Daniel Nashs in the earth today. They are known only to God (and maybe a few family members or friends). They may never write a book. They may never have a television program. They may never have a large public ministry that draws money, popularity, and acclaim of the masses, but their unseen labors in the spirit through intercessory prayer are resulting in the work of God moving forward in the earth. They may be strangers while here, but one day they will be champions in heaven.

> There is no substitute for prayer. There is no shortcut around prayer.

NO SHORTCUTS

There is a holy work in the earth that can only be done in the spirit through intercession for which there is no substitute. Its value cannot be overestimated, for without it very little, if any, eternal benefit, will be gained. Today, many are attempting to offer the world programs, talent, music, and attractive emotional appeals in an effort to sway the hearts of the masses to God. But more often than not, these efforts fall pathetically short of the goal. They simply don't have the spiritual muscle which is always required to see the manifestation of what Jesus was describing when He said, *"Your kingdom come. Your will be done on earth as it is in heaven"* (Matthew 6:10 NKJV). The kingdom of heaven will not invade the earthly realms, destroying the strongholds of demonic darkness, until the people of God intercede and in faith declare it to be so. There is no shortcut to seeing the outpouring of heaven's power in the earth. These things happen the same way they have always happened across the centuries.

79

> Through prayer you have the ability to transform nations!

God's presence, power, and glory will be seen when His people pray with fervent passion, holy conviction, and unwavering perseverance!

A. T. Pierson said, "From the Day of Pentecost, there has not been one great spiritual awakening in any land which has not begun in a union of prayer, though only among two or three. No such outward, upward movement has continued after such prayer meetings have declined."

Early in the Welsh Revival (1904), a Wiltshire evangelist visited the meetings at Ferndale. He stood up and said, "Friends, I have journeyed to Wales with the hope that I may glean the secret of the Welsh Revival." In an instant, Evan Roberts was on his feet, and with an uplifted arm, he said, "My brother, there is no secret! Ask and ye shall receive!"[18] There is no substitute for prayer. There is no shortcut around prayer. John Bunyan once said, "You can do more than pray after you have prayed, but you cannot do more than pray until you have prayed."

AN UNPRECEDENTED HARVEST

In one decade (2000-2009), our ministry – Christ for all Nations, founded by Reinhard Bonnke – saw more than 53 million people receive Jesus as their Savior in our massive evangelistic campaigns in Africa.[19] This incredible harvest of souls did not happen as a result of clever marketing or bizarre publicity stunts. Rather, it is the result of a Holy Spirit outpouring of biblical proportions.

None of us would ever be so naïve as to think that this is our own doing, but we realize that there are many thousands of people around the world who have wept and prayed for us and for the harvest like Daniel Nash prayed for Charles Finney and like the Church prayed for the release of Peter from prison.

The same invisible hands that struck the chains from Peter's wrists are breaking the chains off of nations as we go and preach the gospel in obedience to the Great Commission. None of this would be possible were it not for the persistent and continual prayers of the people of God. We believe that every one of the faithful prayer warriors who have stood at our side and covered us in prayer are just as important as the one preaching on the platform. I believe that those who cover us in prayer will have a share in the rewards because God does not reward according to our function. He rewards according to our faithfulness and obedience.

81

You may never be able to preach to millions of people, minister to kings and governors, or start a worldwide evangelistic ministry, but through prayer **you** have the ability to transform nations. What an incredible thought!

If we desire to see our church, our city, and our nation shaken and the harvest gathered in, we must pray! If we desire to see an outpouring of the Holy Spirit in our time, we must pray! If we want to see the chains that Satan has crafted for our generation fall at our feet, we must pray. If we want to see prison doors open as they did for Peter and the captives set free, we must pray! If we want to see the dam breached and God's glory flood the earth, **we must pray!**

VII

PRAYER
THAT RELEASES
THE MIRACULOUS

And my speech and my preaching
was not with enticing words of man's wisdom,
but in demonstration of the Spirit and of power.
1 Corinthians 2:4

Because God has already rent the heavens through the blood of Jesus and given us access to all of His resources through prayer, we can live and work under an open heaven! Because of this truth, the glory of God is our inheritance as the children of God.

The word "glory" is found throughout the Bible. It can be used in several ways. One example that is found in Scripture is when "glory" is used to describe honor, wealth, and power. This would be like a reference to the "glory" of a king or a person held in high esteem. The second usage of the word is to describe God's manifested or tangible presence. If we carefully examine this definition of "glory," we will discover that it can be used to describe personal encounters that people have in which God's glorious presence moves out of the supernatural realm into the earthly realm.[20] It is experienced by people using one or more of their five natural senses: sight, hearing, taste, touch, and smell. Are we saying that God can be experienced in this way? Yes!

Throughout the Scriptures of the Old and New Testaments, we find examples of times where ordinary people experienced God in these ways. Approximately 2 million of God's people saw His glory with their physical eyes by day as a pillar of cloud and by night as a pillar of fire. This wasn't a mystical or emotional spiritual experience. These people actually **saw** the cloud by day. They **saw** the fire by night. Children who were born in the wilderness grew up never knowing that this manifested, visible revelation of the glory of the Lord was something that was out of the ordinary!

Moses saw and experienced this same holy fire when he stood before a burning bush in Exodus 3:1-6. God spoke to him in this place and even told him, *"Take your sandals off your feet, for the place where you stand is holy ground"* (Exodus 3:5 NKJV). Moses saw the fire of God and experienced something of His holiness as did Isaiah because the Bible says, *"he was afraid to **look** upon God"* (v.6 NKJV).

> The glory of God is our inheritance as the children of God.

Another example of the revelation of the glory of the Lord occurred on the Day of Pentecost. This example involved people physically hearing the sound of His glory as the Holy Spirit was poured out upon those who had gathered. Acts 2:2-3 NKJV records:

> *"And suddenly there came a **sound** [they could hear] from heaven, as of a rushing mighty wind, and it filled the whole house where they were sitting. Then there **appeared** [they could see] to them divided tongues, as of fire, and one sat upon each of them."*

86

The miracles of Jesus were revelations of the glory of the Lord, because they were heavenly invasions that impacted people in ways that they could experience using their natural senses.

In John 2, we find the story of the first miracle Jesus did at a wedding in Cana where something terribly embarrassing for the host family had occurred – they had run out of wine! Mary, the mother of Jesus, came to her Son asking Him to please do something. Jesus commanded the servants to take six large water-pots, each one capable of holding between 20 to 30 gallons, and to fill them with water. They filled them to the brim. When the master of the feast had tested the water, to his utter amazement it had become the finest of wine. This was the first miracle Jesus performed. John recorded the account this way, *"This beginning of signs Jesus did in Cana of Galilee, and **manifested His glory**; and His disciples believed in Him"* (John 2:11 NKJV).

God's power flowed into the earth and six pots of water had been turned into the finest, most exquisite wine as a result of this heavenly intervention.

In Acts 4, we read the account of the intercession of the early Church as they prayed for more boldness to preach the gospel and see powerful demonstrations of the Holy Spirit through signs and wonders. The Bible says, *"And when they had prayed, the place where they were assembled together was **shaken**; and they were all filled with the Holy Spirit, and they spoke the word of God with boldness"* (Acts 4:31 NKJV).

The miracles of Jesus were revelations of the glory of the Lord, because they were heavenly invasions that impacted people in ways they could experience using their natural senses.

87

When these people who had already been filled with the Holy Spirit on the Day of Pentecost prayed for the boldness to preach the gospel without compromise, the glory of God filled the place with such power that even the physical building where they had gathered was shaken! Heaven invaded the house! That's power!

In Acts 5:14-16 NKJV we read that the measure of God's manifest glory was resting upon Peter in a great way:

> *"And believers were increasingly added to the Lord, multitudes of both men and women, so that they brought the sick out into the streets and laid them on beds and couches, that at least **the shadow** of Peter passing by might fall on some of them. Also a multitude gathered from the surrounding cities to Jerusalem, bringing sick people and those who were tormented by unclean spirits, and **they were all healed**."*

It is incredible to think that it is possible to walk in such a measure of the manifest glory of God that no sickness or demonic power would be able to stand in our presence any more than a snowball can withstand the blue flame of a welder's torch!

EXPERIENCING THE GOSPEL

By this definition, God in all of His splendor, can and does move into the natural realm of human existence where He can actually be experienced by people. I believe that people everywhere long to be touched by God in a tangible way. A lost and dying world longs to see the gospel, experience the gospel, and be touched and healed by the power of the gospel. They want to do more than to just hear the gospel with their ears. A person who hears the gospel should have an experience that needs an explanation, not just an explanation of something that is in need of an experience! The gospel must be a life-altering encounter.

Miracles Today

The manifestation of God's glory is not just something that happened in biblical times. Right now, because of the prayers of God's people, faith in His Word, and the declaration of the gospel, we are seeing God's glory manifested all over the world every day.

In the city of Kafanchan in Nigeria, I received a word of knowledge about HIV AIDS, and a young man in the final stages of the disease suddenly fell to the ground under the power of God. That night he dreamt that Jesus came to him and told him that he was healed. He went to the doctor the next morning and was tested again. That evening he brought a report to the meeting. I held it in my hand and read it to the crowd of over 220,000 people – HIV negative! He received a blood transfusion from heaven. Praise the Lord!

> A person who hears the gospel should have an experience that needs an explanation, not just an explanation of something that is in need of an experience.

89

☞ In the city of Nsukka, where more than 425,000 people gathered in the final meeting, Mrs. Regina Attah came with her three children: Umeka (12), Chinwendu (10), and their brother Chukwudi (7). All three children were totally blind; Umeka for eight years, Chinwendu for two years, and little Chukwudi for one year. During the prayer for the sick, all three children received perfect sight at the same moment!

☞ In Isokoland, a girl, deaf and dumb for 20 years, could suddenly hear and speak clearly after receiving prayer. Her brother was standing somewhere in the crowd of more than a quarter million when he saw his sister speaking for the first time in two decades. It was an emotional sight to watch as he ran through the crowd to the platform where they embraced, wept, and rejoiced together.

☞ In Mubi, among the 630,000 people present that night, was one young lady who had been crippled for over 20 years. During the prayer for the sick, she fell on the ground and said that a man surrounded by light wearing a white garment came to her and said, "What do you want?" She said, "I want to be healed." When she awoke, she discovered that she had full use of her legs – she could even run!

☞ In Bali, one lady testified that she was dying from breast cancer; there were open sores across her chest, and her entire right side was paralyzed. When she received her healing, she was not at the meeting. She was lying on her bed at home. But she could hear the preaching coming over the gigantic PA system and blanketing the entire area with the sound of the gospel message. She said she heard me say, "If you are lying on a bed, get up now!" She responded in faith and suddenly she said she felt as though two hands lifted her to her feet. That is when she realized she was no longer paralyzed, the sores on her chest had dried up, and the cancer was gone. She was totally healed! This woman who had been unable to stand before now walked all the way through the massive field where our open-air meeting was taking place and up to the platform to give her testimony.

☞ In Otukpo a man was totally healed after being totally blind in both eyes for over 80 years!

☞ In Rio de Janeiro, Brazil, a lady who had undergone 12 major back surgeries was still confined to a wheelchair. After receiving prayer, she jumped out of the wheelchair, totally healed!

☞ In Sapele I received a word of knowledge about someone who had been wounded by a gunshot and had not been able to recover from it for years. In response to that word, a lady came to the platform to share her story. She had been shot in the leg four years earlier and had been partially crippled since. That night, after prayer, she and I danced together on the platform – she was totally healed!

☞ In Ugep a woman brought her son for prayer who had been totally insane for the last 15 years. He was completely mad, violent, and uncontrollable. After receiving prayer, an amazing transformation took place. He spoke softly and was in his right mind. He told me that Jesus had healed him. Praise the Lord!

☞ In Taraba State in Nigeria, the governor came to see me with his sister who was barren. I prayed for her that God would open her womb and she would become pregnant. When I visited another city in that state one year later, the governor came to see me again with his sister. This time she was nine months pregnant and about to give birth. She gave thanks to God for the miracle. (Pictures of these miracle testimonies can be found on pages 116-123.)

I could go on and on with the testimonies of incredible salvations, healings, deliverances, and miracles that happen **every night** in **every campaign** because of the power of the gospel and the power of prayer offered in faith. In fact, certain pastors have told us that so many miracles took place during the week of our Gospel Campaign that it took the local churches a year to hear all of the testimonies!

RAISED FROM THE DEAD

One of the most incredible miracles we have experienced happened in the city of Onitsha in Nigeria. On November 30, 2001, Daniel Ekechukwu and a friend were in a terrible car accident; they collided with a stone pillar head-on. Daniel's chest was thrust into the steering wheel and his head went through the windshield. He was rushed to the hospital and placed under intensive care where he died soon thereafter. Dr. Josse Annebunwa was the doctor on duty at St. Eunice's Clinic who pronounced Daniel dead that day. He was transferred to the mortuary where he was embalmed. That night his wife, Nneka, began to pray and call upon the name of the Lord. She pleaded with God and reminded Him of His promises to her. Somehow she knew she should not accept her husband's death. She remembered the scripture in Hebrews 11:35 that said, *"Women received their dead raised to life again"*.

Three days later, Nneka asked her father-in-law to let her take her husband's embalmed body to where Evangelist Reinhard Bonnke was preaching. When they arrived at the church, the pastors couldn't decide what to do with the coffin. The local authorities demanded that they open the coffin so they could confirm that it was indeed a corpse and not a bomb. After clearing the coffin, the pastors decided to allow it to be placed in the basement.

Upstairs Evangelist Bonnke was preaching. Downstairs Daniel's wife and father were praying. Slowly, they said, a change began to take place. They witnessed how Daniel began to take shallow breaths even though his body was still stiff from rigor mortis. Other pastors gathered around the body and began massaging it, praying and singing praises to God.

Suddenly Daniel's eyes began moving. He sat up and asked for a drink of water! They said that for weeks afterward his body continued to smell of formaldehyde from the embalming process. But Daniel was raised to life and went on to share his incredible testimony around the world to the glory of God. This extraordinary miracle has been thoroughly documented in the film entitled "Raised from the Dead."[21]

93

AN EXTRAORDINARY CALLING

The Bible is full of accounts of how God has demonstrated His glory throughout history. Some people think that these are only stories that have been passed down for historical reasons and are only intended to entertain us and teach us allegorical lessons.

They are wrong! Others believe that these biblical stories are examples of God's maximum ability. This is also wrong! These testimonies are but a sampling of what is possible in God. With God, the supernatural is natural and the impossible is possible. Christianity is intended to be a supernatural existence from beginning to end, and the demonstration of God's power should be the norm.

> The demonstration of God's power should be the norm.

Someone said to me, "What is your ministry gift?" They thought I would talk about being an apostle, prophet, pastor, teacher, or evangelist. Instead, I said, "I'm an usher." The greatest calling that any of us can have is to usher the presence of God into a world that so desperately needs to experience it. Through prayer, you have the privilege to usher in the glory of God, bringing heaven to earth. Now that is an extraordinary calling!

VIII

PRAYING WITH EXPECTANCY

But let him ask in faith, nothing wavering.
For he that wavereth is like a wave of the sea
driven with the wind and tossed.

James 1:6

The angel suddenly vanished and a cool morning breeze sent a chill down Peter's arm. Suddenly he realized that he was awake and everything he had just experienced was real. The chains had really fallen from his wrists. He had really walked right past the guards. The huge iron gates had really opened and he was really free! Knowing that the believers were praying for him, he made his way through the empty streets to the house of Mary, the mother of John Mark. This is where the prayer meeting was being held, and Peter could hardly wait to show his face to his dear friends who were diligently interceding for his release.

This is where the story becomes a bit comical because while all of the other barriers and doors had opened to Peter so freely, he was about to encounter one door that would not open to him.

The Bible says in Acts 12:13 that Peter knocked at the gate and a young lady named Rhoda heard it. She came to the door, and through the crack she asked, "Who's there?" Peter said, "It's me, Rhoda ... I've just been delivered from prison. Open the door and let me come in." Rhoda was so excited to hear Peter's voice that she failed to open the door. She ran back into the room where the prayer meeting was in full swing. Some were bowing, others were weeping, still others were warring in the heavenlies for Peter's release.

Rhoda interrupted the prayer meeting with the urgent announcement, "Hey, everybody! Peter is at the door." They laughed at her. "You're crazy, Rhoda ... don't you know that Peter is in prison? He is bound between two soldiers, behind two wards of guards, behind a massive iron gate. Peter couldn't possibly be at the door. Now get back in here and pray!"

I'm not sure how long the debate continued, but the Bible does tell us that all the while this discussion was taking place, Peter continued knocking.

What a comical irony! Every door had opened to Peter except the door of the house where the believers were praying for the doors to open. This illustrates a powerful point. God has given us the keys to the kingdom. He has made us the doorkeeper. What we bind in heaven will be bound on earth ... what we loose in heaven will be loosed on earth. We have the power and authority to open every door. There is no power on earth that can stand against us, and the very gates of hell itself will not prevail. But there is one door that can always stand in our way and keep us from receiving our miracle. It is **the door of unbelief**.

> There is one door that can always stand in our way and keep us from receiving our miracle. It is the door of unbelief.

So often the answer to our prayers has been standing on our own front porch, but we have missed it because we did not believe that God had actually heard and answered us. The believers were praying for Peter, but apparently they did not believe that God would answer them. The only thing worse than prayerlessness is prayer without expectation.

Unfortunately, many people think of prayer as being merely a religious exercise that appeases God's need to be talked to. It is a kind of religious duty, like paying a bill that is due. When they pray, they feel better about themselves. When they don't pray, they feel guilty. They seem to think that God keeps a stopwatch and records the minutes they put in, similar to the way a time clock keeps track of employees who are working on their job to receive a paycheck.

Jesus dismissed this mind-set about prayer when He said, *"And when you pray, do not use vain repetitions as the heathen do. For they think that they will be heard for their many words. Therefore do not be like them. For your Father knows the things you have need of before you ask Him"* (Matthew 6:7-8 NKJV).

So if praying long prayers with many words is not the key to receiving an answer – then what is? The answer is simple – **faith!**

THE REAL ENEMY – UNBELIEF

In Matthew 17, we read that a certain man with a demon-possessed son had come to Jesus' disciples for help, but when they could not cast out the evil spirits, they asked Jesus why they had been so unsuccessful. He said to them, *"Because of your unbelief"* (v.20). This is a very clear and precise explanation that Jesus reiterated by going on to say, *"For verily I say unto you, If ye have faith as a grain of mustard seed, ye shall say unto this mountain, Remove hence to yonder place; and it shall remove; and nothing shall be impossible unto you"* (v.20). The simplicity and clarity of this statement is often overshadowed by confusion at the next words out of Jesus' mouth: *"Howbeit this kind goeth not out but by prayer and fasting"* (v.21).

99

> The only thing worse than prayerlessness is prayer without expectation.

It almost sounds as if Jesus had contradicted Himself. When asked why the disciples had not been able to exorcize the demon, He said it was because of unbelief. But now He seems to be saying that it is because they had not fasted and prayed enough. Which is it? The confusion comes when we fail to realize the moral of the story.

At first glance, it may appear that the demon is the focal point of this account, but a closer look will reveal that the real antagonist in this story is not the demon, but the spirit of unbelief. The disciples were concerned about the demon inside the boy, but Jesus was concerned about the unbelief inside His disciples. The disciples' question was about casting out demons, but Jesus' answer was about casting out doubt, because Jesus knew that once unbelief has been cast out, exorcizing demons would be a piece of cake.

Sometimes we have to pray long prayers and fast for many days before we get the victory, but it is not because our appeals coerce God into doing something, twisting His arm through many words. And it is not because we have finally earned the answer to our prayers by logging enough credit hours into our spiritual bank account.

Much fasting and prayer may be necessary and useful in helping us to get the victory over our own stubborn flesh and cast out the spirit of unbelief that blocks God's power from flowing through us. It is this **kind of unbelief** that goes out "but by prayer and fasting." Any way you look at it, faith is the key to powerful prayer. This is the point that Jesus made in this story.

CASTING OUT UNBELIEF

In Matthew 9:25, when Jairus' daughter had died, Jesus had to send everyone out of the room before He could raise her from the dead. Why didn't He allow all those scorning skeptics to see the miracle with their own eyes? Because He had to cast the unbelief out.

> Jesus knew that once unbelief has been cast out, exorcizing demons would be a piece of cake.

Peter did the same thing in Acts 9:40 NASB: *"But Peter sent them all out and knelt down and prayed, and turning to the body, he said, 'Tabitha, arise.' And she opened her eyes, and when she saw Peter, she sat up."* Jesus taught His disciples a lesson: Cast the spirit of unbelief out and nothing will be able to stand against you; demons, death, and even the most formidable mountains will obey your command.

EXPECT TO RECEIVE

In Acts, chapter 3, we read an incredible story about a lame man who happened to be in the right place at the right time:

> *Now Peter and John were going up to the temple at the ninth hour, the hour of prayer.*
> *And a man who had been lame from his mother's womb was being carried along, whom they used to set down every day at the gate of the temple which is called Beautiful, in order to beg alms of those who were entering the temple.*

When he saw Peter and John about to go into the temple, he began asking to receive alms.

But Peter, along with John, fixed his gaze upon him and said, "Look at us!"

And he began to give them his attention, expecting to receive something from them.

But Peter said, "I do not possess silver and gold, but what I do have I give to you: In the name of Jesus Christ the Nazarene – walk!"

And seizing him by the right hand, he raised him up; and immediately his feet and his ankles were strengthened.

With a leap he stood upright and began to walk; and he entered the temple with them, walking and leaping and praising God.

Acts 3:1-8 NASB

There are a couple of things that jump out at me when I read this passage. The first is that it says in verse 3 that this lame man **saw** Peter and John about to go into the temple and **asked** to receive alms, but in verse 4 Peter commands him saying, "Look at us!" It was only afterwards that it says in verse 5, *"He began to give them his attention, **expecting** to receive something from them."*

The lame man had seen Peter and John, but he wasn't paying attention. He had asked for something, but he didn't expect to receive it. Have you ever found yourself coming to the Lord in this way? Have you prayed for something with no expectation that it will ever come

> Without faith your prayer could actually be a sin.

to pass? This was the kind of prayer meeting taking place in Mary's house. Though they prayed for Peter's release, they did not believe it would ever happen – even when Peter himself was standing at the door! Although God had heard their prayers and was willing and able to do what they asked, their own unbelief had blocked the answer.

Without faith your prayer could actually be a sin because Romans 14:23 says that *"whatsoever is not of faith is sin."* Before Peter and John could release the healing power of God into the body of that lame man, they had to get him to change his posture to one of faith and expectancy. That is why the Lord says to you today through His Word, "Look at Me! Pay attention to what I am saying! Expect to receive when you ask!"

James 1:6-8 NKJV says, *"But let him ask in faith, with no doubt, for he who doubts is like a wave of the sea driven and tossed by the wind. For let not that man suppose that he will receive anything from the Lord; he is a double-minded man, unstable in all his ways."*

THE ATMOSPHERE OF EXPECTANCY

In our great evangelistic meetings in Africa, the people come with a high level of spiritual hunger and expectancy of the miraculous power of God. They have heard the testimonies of all that God has done for others, and they believe that God will do the same for them. They know that God is going to show His power and glory in these great meetings, and they come in full expectation that they are going to be the recipients of those blessings.

103

It is this attitude that actually takes hold of the miraculous and causes the lightning of God's glory to strike. They do not come hoping it is the will of God to reveal Himself – they already know it is! Because they already expect this, they pray from a position of bold confidence and expectancy. When God hears that kind of prayer and sees that kind of action being demonstrated by desperately hungry people, He does reveal His awesome power in some of the most phenomenal ways.

Praying with faith and expectancy will always attract the presence and power of God just as the absence of these key elements will repel the presence and power of God. There is a direct correlation between the level of belief and expectancy in the hearts of people and the measure of the revelation of the glory of the Lord. When God's people pray in the firm conviction that it is God's will to answer their prayers and reveal His glory, their expectation of His glory will bring its manifestation in their lives.

Bring your Umbrella

Many years ago, a region of the American Midwest had been stricken by drought. There was a small town there that was totally dependent upon farming, and the crops were dying in the fields because of the lack of rain. A day of prayer and fasting was declared in which all the townspeople would come in from their surrounding farms and spend the day in prayer, asking God to send rain.

That morning a five-year-old girl came along with her parents to their church to pray. Some people were amused as this little girl was carrying an umbrella. They asked her why. She replied that she thought they had come there that day to pray for rain, and she didn't want to get wet going home.

Suddenly conviction gripped their hearts. The people realized that they had come to pray, but no one but this little girl actually believed anything was going to change! In tears, they repented of their unbelief; and these same townspeople began to pray that day as though they really believed their prayers were going to change things.

> Praying with faith and expectancy will always attract the presence and power of God just as the absence of these key elements will repel the presence and power of God.

About four o'clock that afternoon, clouds began to form on the western sky. By evening, a slow, soaking rain had begun to fall across the region. The heavens had literally opened for these people. This slow rain lasted for three days and nights. Their crops were saved, and they eventually had one of the biggest harvests that they had ever seen! Everyone remembered that it was the little girl with her umbrella who had come to pray and had changed their hearts from a place of religious duty bound with unbelief to a place of expectancy that God would in fact hear and act.

We **must** believe and expect God's best blessings whenever we pray!

IX

PREACHING AND PRAYER – A MATCH MADE IN HEAVEN

For as the body without the spirit is dead,
so faith without works is dead also.

James 2:26

nside Mary's house, the prayer meeting had come to a halt and a debate was raging. Some said Peter had been delivered. Others said it was just an apparition standing at the door, but all the while Peter continued knocking.

After all the fasting and prayer had been done, there was still something those faithful intercessors needed to do before they could receive the miracle they so earnestly desired. They had to get off their knees and go answer the door. This is a powerful illustration because the truth is that prayer, while powerful and necessary, is not enough.

> Prayer must be accompanied by action, just like a gun must be equipped with bullets.

Prayer must be accompanied by action, just as a gun must be equipped with bullets. James made the connection when he said, *"Faith without works is dead also"* (James 2:26). Jesus told the disciples to pray for laborers to be sent out into the harvest, and then He turned to those very same men, and said, *"Go into all the world and preach the gospel"* (Mark 16:15 NKJV). The disciples had become the answer to their own prayers!

Evangelist Reinhard Bonnke has asked this question: If every Christian would lock themselves in the prayer closet 24 hours per day, 7 days per week, 365 days per year, and do nothing but pray for the salvation of this world, what would happen? The answer is … nothing. Nothing will happen until someone wakes up in the prayer meeting and goes out into the highways and byways to tell a sinner that Jesus saves!

If you could draw close enough to God to lay your head on His chest and listen to His heartbeat, this is what it would sound like: "Sal-va-tion, Sal-va-tion, Sal-va-tion." God loves the world so much that He sent His only begotten Son who paid the ultimate price to purchase our salvation. Could there be any more ardent explanation of God's deepest desire? How can a person claim that they are intimate with God and yet have no burden for the lost? And how can a person claim to have a burden for the lost and yet do nothing to reach them? The deduction is simple: True intercessors are also soulwinners.

> How can a person claim that they are intimate with God and yet have no burden for the lost?

But the pendulum swings both ways. Any ministry not born out of intimacy is a hoax. God is not looking for hired hands – He is looking for sons and daughters. If prayer is the right leg, the preaching of the gospel is the left leg. One without the other produces a crippled Church. Since God has given us both, there is no need to hobble about, but we can march down the gates of hell when these two ingredients come together.

It's amazing that in some circles there is a rivalry between those called to pray and those called to preach. Those who feel a special calling to pray often think that everyone should be as they are – praying for hours every day and fasting constantly. Those with a special gifting to evangelize think everyone should be standing on street corners with Bibles and bullhorns. But both prejudices are wrong. While it's true that every intercessor must also be a soulwinner and every soulwinner must also be an intercessor, God gives different gifts to different people and we need each other. Actually, it is absolutely imperative that the evangelists and the intercessors work together if we hope to facilitate this great end-time harvest of souls in our generation.

> Every intercessor must also be a soulwinner and every soulwinner must also be an intercessor.

As I mentioned earlier, in just 10 years an astounding 53 million people received Jesus Christ as their Savior during the mass evangelistic events held by our ministry, Christ for all Nations. Nonetheless, I believe that the greatest days of harvest are still ahead of us! Someone once said, "The opportunity of a lifetime must be seized during the lifetime of the opportunity." In order for us to seize the moment that God has given to our generation, it is going to require a strategic, divine alliance between the soul-winners and the intercessors who will unite around the agenda of Jesus – to seek and to save those who are lost.

I believe with all my heart that the greatest move of God in the history of the world is standing on the front porch, knocking on the door. Together we will answer it for Calvary's sake.

THE END

Endnotes

1. John Wesley (1703-1791) is credited as the man that God used to birth what is now called the First Great Awakening in England. He was an Anglican theologian and is the father of Methodism. He was known for emphasizing the doctrine of Christian Perfection and Entire Sanctification. Wesley held the view that in this life Christians could come to a state in which the love of God, or perfect love, reigned supreme in their hearts. Under his ministry he traveled approximately 250,000 miles on horseback preaching the gospel and preached over 50,000 sermons. Towards the end of his life he was widely respected and referred to as "the best loved man in England."

2. Adoniram Judson, Jr. (1788-1850), one of the first American, Baptist, missionaries, is known as the first missionary to Burma where he served for nearly 40 years (in reality he was preceded by other missionaries, but they did not stay very long and their work was not nearly as significant). Judson's work as a missionary led to the formation of the first Baptist association in America. He inspired many Americans to become or support missionaries. Through that support he was able to translate the Bible into Burmese and established several Baptist churches in Burma.

3. David Brainerd (April 20, 1718 - October 9, 1747) was an American missionary to the Native American Indians. His short life, filled with trials and difficulties, produced lasting fruit among the tribes where he ministered. Brainerd's biography entitled "An Account of the Life of the late Reverend Mr. David Brainerd", was published in 1749 by Jonathan Edwards and the story of his life and ministry has inspired countless other missionaries throughout succeeding generations. Brainerd is considered part of an influential class of missionaries who stand out in history as pioneers and trailblazers in the modern missions movement.

4. John "Praying" Hyde (1865-1912) was an American Missionary to India. His father was also in the ministry and prayed both in his church and his home that laborers would be sent to the mission fields. John himself became an answer to that prayer. The Indian nationals called him "the man who never sleeps" because of his long sessions of prayer, which is how he earned the name "Praying Hyde." He helped lead hundreds of souls to Christ in India and the in influence of his prayers and ministry

can still be felt throughout the sub-continent today. While still a young man, in his forties, John Hyde's health began to fail as a result of his extraordinary work. The doctors told him that unless he rested, death would be the outcome, but he persisted preaching and praying until he was forced to return to America in 1911. While passing through Wales he became friends with G. Campbell Morgan who later said that he had learned what true prayer was from "Praying Hyde". His dying words were "Shout the victory of Jesus Christ!"

5. Bits & Pieces, May 28, 1992, page 15

6. Milner-White, Eric, "A Procession of Passion Prayers" (London: Oxford University Press, 1941) page 23

7. Vine, W. E., "Vine's complete Expository Dictionary of Old and New Testament Words", (Nashville: Thomas Nelson Publishing, 1996) page 406

8. A light-year is the distance light travels (over 186,000 miles per second) in a year; approximately 6 trillion miles.

9. This Scientific Information has been verified by Dr. Richard Tresch Fienberg, Press Officer and Education & Outreach Coordinator, American Astronomical Society

10. Ludwig A. Kolenda (1859-1923), is the great grandfather of the author. He was a successful dairy farmer and pastored a church in his home in Germany until he was invited to move to Brazil at age 43 to be a missionary among the German settlers there. He moved his family again to the USA to begin church planting in 1902 and received the baptism of the Holy Spirit when the Pentecostal revival swept through the USA in the early 1900's. All during his missions, and pastoral work he supported his family by farming.

11. John P. Kolenda (1899-1984), is the great great uncle of the author. John was born to a German Lutheran Missionary and church planter. After one of his brothers attended and received the experience of the baptism of the Holy Spirit at an Amy McPherson meeting, and returned home to tell the home church about this great new outpouring. John was also baptized in the Holy Spirit and felt called to return back to the areas his father had established churches in Brazil and Germany. In addition to pastoring churches in Michigan, John founded Bible schools in Germany and Brazil that are still active today. Among many around the world, he is still affectionately referred to as "Opa".

12. John P. Kolenda, "Vater geht aufs Ganze", (Leuchter-Verlag GmbH, 6106 Erzhausen), page 75

13. Vine, W. E., "Vine's Complete Expository Dictionary of Old and New Testament Words", (Nashville: Thomas Nelson Publishing, 1996), page 523

14. Betzalel, Israel B. "Teaching Messiah from the Torah", The Jerusalem Council, 2010. www.jerusalemcouncil.org/articles/commentaries

15. Actual Hebrew translation is "tripper" or "supplanter" which are words best relating to deceiver. Story of his life begins in Genesis 25. Tenney, Merrill C. "The Zondervan Pictorial Bible Dictionary", (Grand Rapids: Zondervan Publishing, 1963) page 398

16. Shiver, John D., "Revival Glory", (Columbus: TEC Publications, 2007), page 28

17. McClymond, Michael, "The Encyclopedia of Religious Revivals in America-Volume 1, (Westport: Greenwood Press, 2007), page 169

18. From an unpublished account of the Welsh Revival, quoted by Arthur Wallis, In the Day of Thy Power, page 112

19. CfaN has counted and recorded every registered decision card in there meetings since 1987. In the last decade alone (between the years 2000-2009) there have been 53 million registered decisions for Christ around the world.

20. Vine, W. E., "Vine's complete Expository Dictionary of Old and New Testament Words", (Nashville: Thomas Nelson Publishing, 1996), page 267

21. DVD "Raised from the Dead", ©2013, Christ for all Nations INC, USA.

Evangelists Daniel Kolenda and Reinhard Bonnke at Otukpo, Nigeria in 2009.

His doctor's report confirmed the miracle: HIV positive turned to HIV negative!

Brother embraced his sister
after she was miraculously healed.

Cancer had paralyzed her –
until Jesus healed her!

A mother praises God for her son's sanity, miraculously restored.

Jesus healed her from a gunshot wound.

A young woman crippled for 20 years is overjoyed at her healing.

A mother's three children simultaneously received sight!

A man was totally healed after being blind in both eyes for over 80 years!

Even after twelve back surgeries, this lady was still confined to a wheelchair ...
until she received a miracle from Jesus!

Raised from the dead! Nneka embraces her husband,
after he was miraculously brought back to life.

The harvest truly is great, but the labourers are few: pray ye therefore the Lord of the harvest, that he would send forth labourers into his harvest.

Luke 10:

Mubi, Nigeria

Yola, Nigeria
Nsukka, Nigeria
Nnewi, Nigeria
Warri, Nigeria
Ugep, Nigeria
Papua New Guinea
Umuahia, Nigeria
Sapele, Nigeria
Ogoja, Nigeria
Okene, Nigeria
Takum, Nigeria
Taipei, Taiwan
Mbuji Mayi, Congo
Oshogbo, Nigeria
Otukpo, Nigeria
Orlu, Nigeria
Lagos Millenium, Nigeria
Uromi, Nigeria
Ogbomosho, Nigeria
Lome, Togo
Wukari, Nigeria
Numan, Nigeria
Ondo, Nigeria
Lagos, Nigeria
Port Harcourt, Nigeria
Mubi, Nigeria

Over 53 million recorded decisions for Christ from 2000 to 2009

Kochin, India

Kiev, Ukraine

Jimma, Ethiopia

Ile Ife, Nigeria

Afikpo, Nigeria

Ikot Ekpene, Nigeria

Goiânia, Brazil

Kabba, Nigeria

Kafanchan, Nigeria

Sydney, Australia

Ijebu Ode, Nigeria

Jalingo, Nigeria

Jos, Nigeria

Khartoum, Sudan

Benin, Nigeria

Isokoland, Nigeria

Hong Kong

Abakaliki, Nigeria

Bali, Nigeria

Agbor, Nigeria

Awka, Nigeria

Ado Ekiti, Nigeria

Aba, Nigeria

Kaduna, Nigeria

Abuja, Nigeria

Calabar, Nigeria

RAISED
FROM
THE
DEAD

A 21st Century
Miracle Resurrection Story

As Reinhard Bonnke debated whether or not to move his ministry to America, he did something he had never done before: he prayed for a sign to confirm that God truly was calling him to go to America. God was about to answer that prayer. THE VERY NEXT DAY, in a Nigerian church where Bonnke was preaching, a woman brought the partially embalmed body of her dead husband. She was praying for a miracle...What happened next is the unbelievable true story of a man brought back to life. Find out the whole chain of events that led to this astounding miracle, and prepare to be amazed at what God can do!

Raised from the Dead available in book or DVD

*Learn more at **CfaN.org***

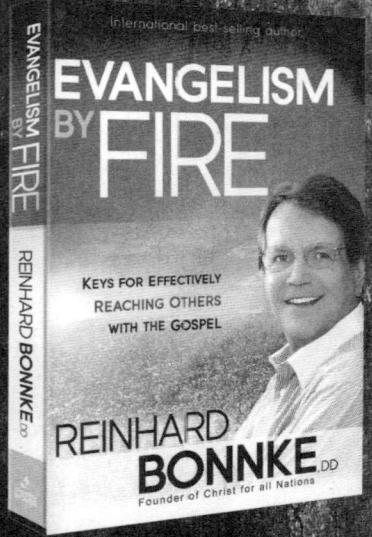

Hell Empty – Heaven Full

Hell was never designed for the Lost.

In Hell Empty – Heaven Full Reinhard Bonnke reveals his personal passion for sharing the Gospel with God's children. He invites you - indeed urges you - to join Jesus at the crossroads between despair and delight. Every day, millions of people move further down the dark road to destruction. Yet one individual, his arms outstretched in the shape of a cross, stands in the middle of that road, blocking their way. His name is Jesus. And one person at a time, he turns the crowds around, gently pointing each one toward an eternity of hope and joy.

There isn't a moment to lose. Hell was never designed for the lost. Heaven is expecting them!

Daniel Kolenda tackles the questions we all have when seeking our purpose. Your life was meant to change the course of world history. Anything less is below what God has for you.
—**Banning Liebscher**, Jesus Culture director

[Wake up to God's will for your life]

LIVE before you die

DANIEL KOLENDA
President of Christ for all Nations

Foreword by REINHARD BONNKE, DD

LIVE before you die   [Wake up to God's will for your life]   DANIEL KOLENDA

Foreword by REINHARD BONNKE DD
DANIEL KOLENDA

PASSIO

GOD IS READY...
ARE YOU READY TO LIVE HIS ADVENTURE FOR YOU?

In *Live Before You Die,* Daniel Kolenda draws from Scripture and his own experiences to help you discover and follow God's call. With advice that is both practical and inspiring Evangelist Kolenda reveals:

- **Five secrets to discovering God's will**
- **How to start moving in the right direction**
- **What to do when God says wait**
- **How to stay in the will of God**

Scan this
QR Code
to purchase
from Amazon

GET YOUR COPY AT AMAZON.COM OR YOUR LOCAL BOOKSTORE

CHRIST FOR ALL NATIONS

To contact Christ for all Nations, the ministry of
Evangelists Reinhard Bonnke and Daniel Kolenda,
please visit our website **www.cfan.org** or use this information:

INT'L HEADQUARTERS

United States
Post Office Box 590588
Orlando, FL 32859-0588
Toll-free: 1 888 800 2757
Phone: 407 854 4400
E-Mail: USA@CfaN.org

Continental Europe
Melsunger Str. 1
60389 Frankfurt am Main
Germany
Phone: +49 69 478 78 0
E-Mail: cfan@bonnke.net

United Kingdom
Highway House, 250 Coombs Rd.
Halesowen, West Midlands B62 8AA
Phone: +44 121 602 2000
E-Mail: info@CfaN.org.uk

Canada
Post Office Box 24090
London, Ontario N6H 5C4
Toll-free: 1 800 459 3709
Phone: 519 432 5723
E-Mail: Canada@CfaN.org

Australia/Pacific
Locked Bag 50
Burleigh Town QLD 4220
Phone: +61 755 082 914
E-Mail: Australia@CfaN.org

Southeast Asia
Singapore Post Centre Post Office
Post Office Box 418
Singapore 914014
Phone: +65 6345 9880
E-Mail: Singapore@CfaN.org

Southern Africa
Post Office Box 50015
West Beach 7449
Phone: +27 21 554 1892/8
E-Mail: SouthAfrica@CfaN.org

Hong Kong
PO Box 97505
Tsim Sha Tsui Post Office
Phone: +852 3904 3000
E-Mail: HongKong@CfaN.org

West Africa
PO Box 10899 Ikeja
Lagos, Nigeria, West Africa
Phone: +234 1 497 1575
E-Mail: cfan@alpha.linkserve.com

Brazil
Avenida Sete de Septembro
Salas 1606-1609
Curitiba - PR CEP 80240-000
Phone: +55 41 3243 7600
E-Mail: LatinAmerica@CfaN.org

This product and other titles published by CfaN are available in other languages.

For more information on the various languages or for international publishing information,
please contact us at publications@cfan.org